' on or be

**Which Form of
Building Contract**

# Which Form of Building Contract

David Chappell

Architecture Design and Technology Press
London

First published in 1991 by
Architecture Design and Technology Press
128 Long Acre
London WC2E 9AN

An imprint of Longman Group UK Limited

British Library Cataloguing in Publication Data
A CIP record for this book is available from the British Library

ISBN 1 85454 950 2

Printed in Great Britain by The Bath Press

# Contents

# Which Form of Building Contract

David Chappell

Architecture Design and Technology Press
London

First published in 1991 by
Architecture Design and Technology Press
128 Long Acre
London WC2E 9AN

An imprint of Longman Group UK Limited

British Library Cataloguing in Publication Data
A CIP record for this book is available from the British Library

ISBN 1 85454 950 2

Printed in Great Britain by The Bath Press

# Preface

Responsibility for advising the client on the most appropriate form of contract lies squarely with the architect or with the professional who is carrying out the architect's functions. He is the person who is going to administer the contract. The client or his solicitor is not sufficiently well versed in construction matters to make the decision without advice. It is essential, therefore, that the architect is familiar with the alternative standard forms available. This may seem extremely tedious, but it has to be done. Looked at purely from the standpoint of self-preservation, an architect who advises his client to use a form of contract which is inappropriate and as a direct result the client suffers loss, will be open to an action for negligence. Put simply, it is part of the architect's duty to know about building contracts.

There is always a temptation to use a familiar form even if another seems more appropriate. In every case, the correct rather than the most 'comfortable' form should be used. This book deals only with standard forms of building contract. It cannot be totally comprehensive, but all the standard forms in common use are included. I decided against including any engineering forms, because rather different criteria are involved and there are large numbers of such forms for various purposes. The book would have doubled in size without appreciably increasing its value to members of the building industry.

The book operates on two levels. The intention is to provide a guide to the principles of contract selection and also to provide a quick method of contract choice by means of charts and tables. Some building projects are carried out using the employer's own form of contract specially drafted by his solicitor. I cannot recommend such contracts for reasons which will become apparent as you read this book. It is possible to carry out amendments to the standard forms, but it is not usually desirable. Some typical amendments are discussed in Chapter 7.

A book like this is crammed with information. It also includes my opinions. I have attempted to look at the criteria, methods of procurement and contract forms objectively, but inevitably I have had to take a view on many aspects.

For ease of writing I have used the male pronoun throughout and, therefore, 'he' can also be read as 'she', 'him' as 'her', etc. The person administering the contract has usually been referred to as the architect because the standard forms make that assumption. It is recognized, however, that the architect's function is sometimes carried out by a building surveyor or even an engineer. It is hoped that this book will prove useful to all construction professionals who give advice about the correct form of building contract for a particular situation.

Throughout the formulation, writing and checking of this book I have benefited from the help and advice of Allan Ashworth MSc ARICS.

*David Chappell*

The standard forms of contract have been abbreviated in the text as follows:

The JCT Standard Form of Building Contract 1980: JCT 80
The JCT Intermediate Form of Building Contract: IFC 84
The JCT Agreement for Minor Building Works: MW 80
The JCT Standard Form of Building Contract With Contractor's
    Design 1981: JCT 81
The Standard Form of Management Contract 1987: JCT 87
The ACA Form of Building Agreement 1982, 1984 edn: ACA 2
The ASI Building Contract: ASI
The ASI Small Works Contract: ASI SW
The ASI Minor Works Contract: ASI MW

# 1 Principles

**1.1**
**Introduction**

It is perfectly possible to carry out a building project on the basis of a simple exchange of letters or even an oral exchange. The basic ingredients for a legally binding contract are that there should be agreement between the parties and that there should be some consideration, or in other words each party should effectively give something to the other. Agreement is usually achieved by the process of offer and acceptance. The builder offers to carry out the work shown on a drawing for a sum of money and the employer accepts the offer. For very small jobs where the builder is well known, the system may work well, but for most building work, a more formal contractual arrangement must be entered into by the parties. A number of standard forms of contract have been devised to suit varying circumstances and to cover the many anticipated situations which can arise during the carrying out of the work.

It is trite to say that no two building projects are the same. Even so, it has to be said. Some building projects are similar, some are wildly different. Standard building contracts are prepared for specific circumstances. It is inviting trouble to use one standard form for every project, and yet there are many architects who do just that or perhaps limit their repertoire to two standard forms.

The fundamental decision sequence which leads to choice of the most suitable form of contract.

The employer will have, as part of his brief, a number of requirements which can be categorised as procurement criteria to differentiate them from the criteria from which the architect will prepare the design for the project. These criteria will range from notions of time and cost to the risk involved and the quality required for the design and construction. Some aspects will be an intrinsic part of the architect's work such as size, design, complexity, or otherwise, of the project. It is clear that a building society which requires a new headquarters might well need it for a certain date. The quality of design must probably be what is generally referred to as 'prestigious'. The society might want to keep close control of the work and the building will be large and complex. After appropriate consultation, usually it would be for the architect to suggest the most suitable means of achieving the required result and the most suitable form of contract to apportion rights and obligations. Whatever form it is decided to use, it should be a different form from the one the architect would recommend for carrying out some refurbishment work to turn a listed building into a residential home for elderly people where the work is rather uncertain, cost is a critical factor and time may not be so important. The criteria are different. Criteria are discussed in detail in Chapter 2.

**1.2**
**Methodology**
There are very many good books available which deal with building procurement and forms of building contract. Some of them are listed in the bibliography at the end of this book. Usually, however, they provide the reader with little more than a description of the alternative methods which are available and typical circumstances under which they may be used. This book offers a pathway through the maze of alternatives. The system adopted should be clear from a glance at the table of contents. The method is explained in detail in Chapter 7, together with examples to show how the system works.

**1.3**
**Procurement systems**
There are fashions in procurement just as in anything else. By way of illustrating the point Fig. 1.1 shows how the use of certain common systems has changed over a recent two year period. At the time of writing, it appears that management contracting and design and build are very popular for large projects. That is not the same as saying that these systems are always chosen correctly of course. It is essential to determine the most appropriate procurement system or systems for any set of criteria before proceeding to select the most suitable form of contract.

**1.4**
**Forms of contract**
There is a variety of standard forms available within the construction industry. The choice of a particular form will depend upon a number of considerations such as:
- Private employer or local authority.
- Method of procurement.
- Source of design input.
- Size of project.
- Allocation of risk.

**1**  Principles

- Type of work.
- Type of documentation.

Although the general content of many of the standard forms is similar, in that they all include clauses dealing with such topics as extensions of time, termination, arbitration and so on, there are many differences in detail and in the inclusion or exclusion of particular contract provisions. The danger indeed is that two totally different forms may be confused because they have a superficial resemblance, for example JCT 80 and JCT 81.

**Fig. 1.1**

Changes in procurement systems – percentage of contracts by value.

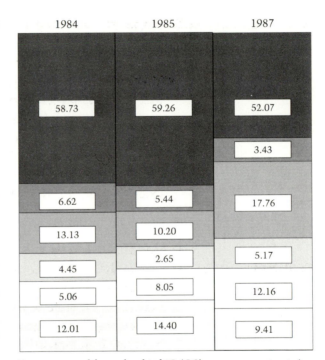

Data extracted from the third JO (QS) survey – contracts in use 1987 published in *Chartered Quantity Surveyor*, January 1989.

The choice of available standard forms is increasing and the existing forms are regularly updated by either complete revision or by the issue of amendments to take account of requests from the industry, case law developments or changes in practice.

There are dangers in making 'homemade' amendments to standard forms. Although it may sometimes be sensible to amend a form to cater for a particular situation (see Chapter 7), such amendments should always be carried out with great care by a building contract specialist. Some of the problems which

**1.4   Forms of contract**

can arise as a result of badly considered amendments are:

- Inconsistency of amendments with existing provisions.
- Unknowing transfer of risks as a result of incorrect phrasing.
- Interpretation of the amendment *contra proferentem* (against the maker of the amendment) in the case of ambiguity.

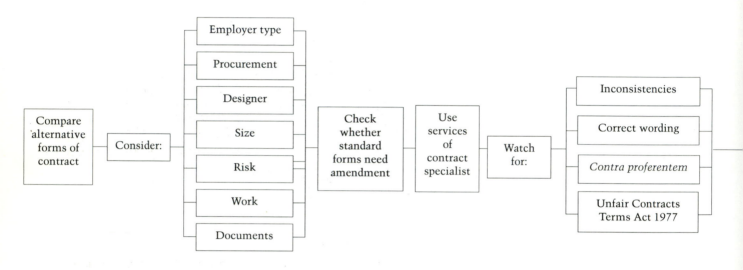

General principles in considering the alternative forms of contract.

- Ineffectiveness of the amendment as a result of the operation of the Unfair Contract Terms Act 1977, because the amendment is construed as an exclusion or restriction of liability.
- Important terms may be omitted.

**1.5**
**General matters**

### 1.5.1 Consultants v contractors

Only the most foolhardy employer or one with specialist construction knowledge within his own organisation will enter into building operations without the benefit of an independent consultant. This is the case even where design and build contracts are employed and JCT 81 makes provision for an 'Employer's Agent' who can be, and usually is, a professional of one kind or another.

**1**  Principles

Design and build can be carried out without the services of an independent consultant and even when a consultant is engaged, there is some difference of view regarding the respective merits of consultant or contractor driven projects. Assuming no consultant is engaged by the employer to advise in relation to a design and build project, the advantages may be:

- More likely to finish on time.
- Price certainty and little likelihood of claims.
- Single point responsibility.
- Buildability.
- Designers and builders act as a team.
- Price includes design fee.

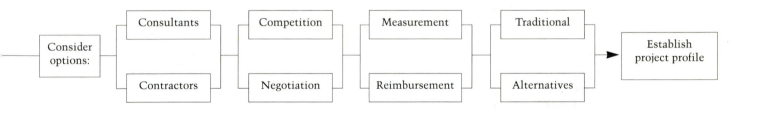

Disadvantages could be said to be:

- Contractor's proposals may not match the employer's requirements.
- Uncertain amount or type of work included in the price.
- Employer's changes of mind are likely to be more costly than with a traditional contract.
- Design quality may suffer.
- Although design fees are not separate, they are included as part of the total price to the employer.
- Lack of independent monitoring of quality, progress and payments. In practice a consultant is usually employed for this purpose and to assist the employer in administration and formulating his requirements.

**1.5.2 Competition v negotiation**
In general, contracts are let on the basis of competition, price, (sometimes) time and (less often) quality, between interested contractors. Usually, that kind of arrangement results in the best deal for the employer, at least in the area open to competition. Thus, competition on price will generally secure the lowest price, but not perhaps the best quality of workmanship from the tenderers.

**1.5** General matters

Even where a negotiated approach is chosen, some element of competition is frequently used to select the contractor most suitable for negotiation. Such a procedure is termed two-stage tendering. Negotiation may be appropriate if:

- There is a business relationship between the parties.
- An early start on site is required.
- A continuation contract (see Chapter 3) is desired.
- Market forces so dictate.
- A contractor with certain attributes is required.
- The geographical area and/or size of project do not make competition a viable proposition.
- Particular financial arrangements are desired.

The factors are indicative only. Nothing can replace assessing each situation on its merits. Among other things, successful negotiation depends on:

- Quality of negotiators.
- Quality of information.
- Determination on both sides to reach agreement.
- Agreement on the basis of negotiation.
- Agreement on basic rates and prices.

### 1.5.3 Measurement v reimbursement

Essentially, there are only two ways of calculating the cost of construction works:

- The work carried out by the contractor is measured and priced in accordance with a rate he has quoted; or
- The contractor is reimbursed his actual costs.

For example, a contract based on specification and drawings relies upon the contractor measuring and pricing the work even although he may only disclose a single lump sum to the employer, at least at tender stage. Such a contract allows payment to the contractor for the risk he takes. Under a reimbursement contract, the contractor has little or no financial risk and the method of payment reflects this. The contractor receives only what he expends together with a sum, however calculated, to cover profit.

There are significant differences between cost reimbursement and measurement contracts in the following respects:

- Contract sum – Only available with measurement contracts. The best which can be achieved with a cost reimbursement contract is a guide price.
- Final price forecast – Only available with measurement contracts which make limited use of provisional quantities.

- Efficiency incentives – Automatically included within a measurement contract. They may have to be inserted as special provisions in cost reimbursement contracts, for example target costs.
- Risk – Measurement contracts will normally include the price of the risk which is payable no matter what the outcome. Claims may arise because risk has been improperly assessed.
- Cost control – The employer has limited control if cost reimbursement is being used.
- Administration – Greater burden of clerical work and record keeping with cost reimbursement contracts.

### 1.5.4 Traditional v alternatives

Until comparatively recently, virtually all building contracts were constructed using traditional procurement methods, which means that the employer commissions an architect to design a building, possibly a quantity surveyor is engaged to produce bills of quantities, and a contractor tenders competitively for the work. The work then proceeds on site with the architect inspecting and carrying out certain functions under the contract, the quantity surveyor measuring and valuing, and so on. Criticisms can be levelled on the following grounds:

- The service may not always be appropriate.
- From inception to completion may be a long time.
- Projects frequently overrun the contract period.
- Final accounts may be unexpectedly higher than forecasted.
- Quality control can be difficult.
- Design may not be practical.
- Legal liabilities are diverse and may be confused.

The alternative procurement systems which have sprung up attempt to address one or more of these difficulties. Methods of procurement are described in Chapter 3, but the following issues must be taken into account:

- Project size.
- Costs, including the design.
- Time from inception to completion.
- Responsibilities.
- Design.
- Standard of quality required.
- Complexity of project.
- Organisation.
- Allocation of risk.
- Financial provisions.

**1.5**   General matters

**1.6**
**Procurement management**

This is the art of setting up the most appropriate system for getting the building built. Traditionally the role, along with many other functions, has been carried out by the architect, but this may not always be the case. Other construction professionals, or the contractor himself, may take the role depending on circumstances. The process of procurement management includes the following:

- Determining the employer's procurement criteria.
- Assessing project viability.
- Advising the most suitable organisational structure.
- Advising the appointment of consultants and contractor.
- Managing information and co-ordinating the activities of the consultants and the contractor from inception to completion.

# 2 Procurement criteria

**2.1**
**Introduction**

The selection of appropriate contract arrangements for any but the simplest project is difficult owing to the large range of options. Choosing a procurement system means eliminating as many options as possible and making a reasoned choice from what remains. In order to make any choice, criteria must be established.

All building projects are different in minor and sometimes in major ways. The differences result from the employer's requirements. Certain requirements have a direct relationship to the type of procurement system and form of contract which should be used in a given situation. These requirements are the procurement criteria. It is not sufficient to say that a criterion is, for example, time, because time has many facets. The employer may be a developer who wants the building erected in the shortest possible time. Alternatively, he may be a supermarket owner whose principal concern is that the building is ready on the pre-arranged date.

Procurement criteria, if they are to be useful, must be carefully defined and qualified. In particular, priorities must be established and qualifications imposed even to the extent of operating a simple ratings system. Great care must be taken over this part of the process, because it is the foundation for what follows. It should be obvious, but in practice appears not to be so, that if the procurement criteria are wrong or wrongly emphasised, the procurement system is likely to be wrong also. Just as the employer will find himself in trouble if he changes the kind of accommodation he requires after the design has been completed, he will find himself in similar trouble if he changes any of his procurement criteria after the procurement arrangements have been finalised.

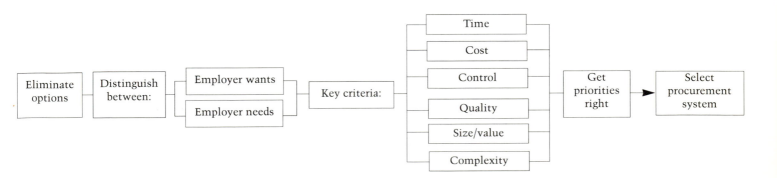

Establishment of procurement criteria.

**2.1** Introduction

**2.2**
**Employer's requirements**

It is essential to separate the employer's wants from his needs. Only if that is successfully achieved is there any chance of avoiding changes of mind at a late stage. For example, when considering their requirements for a new surgery complex, a group of doctors may want a patient waiting area of specified large size. In fact, this requirement may be based on problems encountered in the existing surgery due to an antiquated layout. What is needed may be a smaller waiting area of a different design together with a reorganisation of the appointment system. This is an example based on design and organisation. However, it can also affect procurement, because whether a waiting area is considered to be too large will depend as much on quality of design and finishes as on actual size. Size will affect cost and the time necessary to complete the project. It is clearly not possible in practice simply to consider procurement criteria in isolation. However, when all the requirements have been set down, it is necessary to separate out the procurement criteria in order to begin the process of selection in a logical way. The key criteria are as follows, each one having two facets:

- Time
  -Economy
  -Certainty
- Cost
  -Economy
  -Certainty
- Control
  -Risk to employer
  -Risk to contractor
- Quality
  -Design
  -Construction
- Size/value
  -Medium–large
  -Small–medium
- Complexity
  -Complex
  -Simple

The employer may have conflicting requirements such as quick completion, high quality, large size, high complexity and economy. In other words, the best of all possible worlds. This will be the norm and, therefore, it is important to determine priorities. In order to do that, the key criteria must be properly understood.

2   Procurement criteria

**2.3**
**Key procurement criteria**

### 2.3.1 Time

Once they have made the decision to build, the majority of employers want to see the project completed as quickly as possible. Design and construction processes are known to be lengthy. The time available will influence other things such as the type of design and construction. If speed is the most important of the criteria, standardised designs and construction techniques might be chosen which might reflect adversely on quality.

There is always an absolutely minimum time period for carrying out any project from inception to completion. Identifying just what this period is for any particular project can be a problem. What is certain is that such a period is directly related to the other criteria so that economies in time can only be achieved by sacrificing in other areas: small simple buildings are quicker to erect than large complex buildings; after a certain point, speed becomes very expensive, high speed is often high risk for the employer; and so on.

In order to produce economies in time it may be possible to reduce the period from inception to tender stage, and it may be possible to reduce the period required for operations on site. In practice, the greatest economies in time are usually achieved by telescoping the first period into the second so that the construction starts before all the design and production information is ready. Such arrangements are usually termed fast tracking or fast building. Early selection of the contractor is normally a key factor. From one point of view it can be considered bad practice, because where work begins before details are finalised the employer has less control over the project, and cannot be certain precisely how much it will cost. The contractor will usually be involved in the design stage and that will probably mean a negotiated tender which will generally be more expensive than competitive tendering. But if speed is vital, all other considerations are less important.

If speed is of the essence, the organisation of both design and construction work assumes increased importance. Whether the organisation should be left in its present state, fragmented between architect and contractor or whether it should be in the hands of one or the other or indeed a third party becomes a crucial question. On the principle that more things are achieved when there are fewer people involved in the act of achieving, it is likely that traditional procurement systems should be avoided if time is of the essence. A system which gives the organisational power into the hands of one person is required.

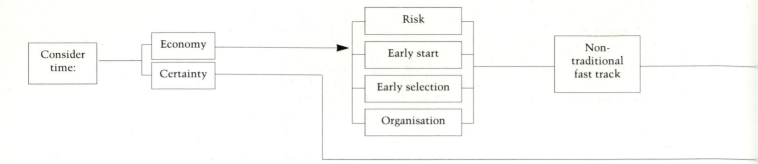

The 'time' factor in establishing procurement criteria.

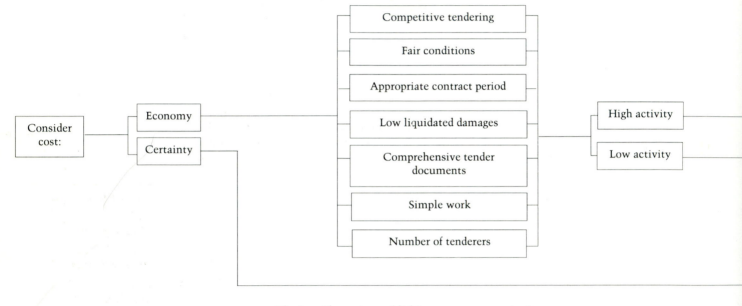

The 'cost' factor in establishing procurement criteria.

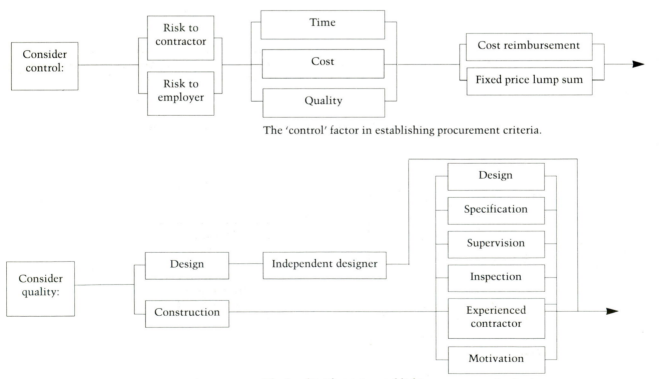

The 'control' factor in establishing procurement criteria.

The 'quality' factor in establishing procurement criteria.

Single purpose

Management

Interlocking working

Information flow

Quality control

Fixed criteria

Information flow

Control

Cost certainty

Cost reimbursement

Traditional tendering

Consider long-term costs:

Life-cycle costing

Lump sum

Cost controls

Strict conditions

High liquidated damages

Consider size/value:

Not conclusive

Indicative only

Dependent on complexity

The 'size and value' factor in establishing procurement criteria.

Consider complexity:

Complex

Simple

Employer

Design

Construction

Site

Phasing

Two-stage tender

Traditional or design and build

The 'complexity' factor in establishing procurement criteria.

This might be the architect, project manager or contractor depending upon other considerations.

The following are among the essential attributes of fast building:

- Unity of purpose.
- Competent management of all stages of work.
- Smoothly interlocking working practices.
- Proper flow of information.
- Effective quality control systems.

Very often, the essential requirement with regard to time is that the completion date is achieved. This is time certainty. It may not matter how long it takes to get to the completion date provided that completion date within reason is certain. A supermarket chain will have to plan for the launch of a new store many months before completion. A delay of even a few days may be disastrous. In those circumstances, an employer will often be advised to opt for a fast building contract, but it should not be overlooked that a traditional arrangement, together with a contract which puts most of the risk on the contractor, can work very well, at a price.

One of the main reasons why contracts do not finish on time is because the employer changes his mind at a late stage or even during the construction process. Another common reason is shortage of production information which may be due to employer changes of mind. If the employer desires time certainty, he must be made to understand that it is incompatible with changes of mind. If the employer settles his requirements, the architect produces full and accurate information, and there are no variations during the progress of the works, the contractor's principal excuses for not completing on time are removed.

With time certainty, control goes in the hands of the employer, with most of the risk residing with the contractor; there is also certainty, but not necessarily economy, of cost. The quality, size and complexity of the project should have no effect other than to fix the completion date nearer to or further from the date of inception. They will not affect the chances of meeting such date when fixed.

### 2.3.2 Cost

If maximum economy of cost is required, some kind of competitive tendering is indicated. In general, open tendering will result in lower tenders than selective tendering, but there will be disadvantages caused by the inclusion of unsuitable or unknown firms. There are other, quite separate, factors which tend to increase the cost of building at tender stage:

- Contract conditions onerous to the contractor.
- High standards of workmanship and materials required.
- Unduly short contract period.
- High liquidated damages provisions.
- Lack of comprehensive tender documents.
- Complexity of the work.
- Restrictions on working hours or space or sequence of working.
- Lack of adequate number of firms on the tender list who are actually prepared to tender, as opposed to simply giving a cover price. In extreme cases it has been known for only one firm actually to tender, with the other firms obtaining a cover price from it.

It is a mistake to concentrate merely on the lowest tender cost of the works if other factors, generally encountered during the progress of the works and which can produce large cost increases on the tender sum, are neglected. Such factors include:

- Employer's changes of mind and consequent variations.
- Late supply of essential information from the architect.
- Fluctuations provisions.
- Interference on site by the employer.
- Employer's defaults resulting in contractor's claims for loss and/or expense.
- Type and amount of cash flow arrangements.

Procurement methods can have a significant effect upon cash flow and, therefore, on the real cost to the employer. If the employer can choose a system which will delay or reduce the size of his first payments to the contractor, it will be advantageous. The speculative development is a good example of this. It is used extensively for housing, factories and offices, and the employer effectively pays for the work by a single payment upon completion of the project. In times of full order books, however, contractors may well decline such arrangements or load the tender accordingly. In appropriate circumstances, a straightforward cost reimbursement contract can be the cheapest way to build. The risk, however, is with the employer and there is no cost certainty. Appropriate circumstances include:

- Complex work of uncertain nature or extent.
- Effective cost controls and recording arrangements.
- Well-organised and competent contractor.
- When contractors, generally, have full workloads.

## 2.3 Key procurement criteria

When prices for construction work are at a low level, a form of cost reimbursement or management fee approach may prove to be an expensive proposition. In times of low construction activity, contractors are sometimes prepared to price the work with a low profit element and take the chance that nothing of significance will go wrong. In times of full workloads, the opposite tends to be the case and paying contractors their actual costs plus an agreed amount for profit may be a better financial solution.

Looked at from a broader standpoint, the employer should be advised on the long-term life-cycle costs of his building. This will affect quality considerations (high-quality construction using durable materials should require less maintenance and, therefore, less expenditure over a long period) and may influence the type of design and even the time spent in construction. Only after a full life-cycle costing exercise has been carried out and all costs expressed in terms of present costs can it be determined whether it is more economical in the long term to invest more in the capital cost of the building. Even if this is shown to be the most cost-effective option, the employer may decide that he does not have the necessary finance.

An employer may be more concerned with cost certainty than cost economy, because he may have a fixed sum to spend which cannot be exceeded under any circumstances. Such a requirement will clearly rule out any kind of cost reimbursement contract. Some kind of lump sum contract is indicated, with strict cost controls. All the factors noted above which must be considered in connection with achieving the lowest possible cost will make the final cost uncertain. It will be noted that it is not enough simply to stipulate that the contract is on a firm price basis. Certainty, unlike economy, of cost should be achievable without influencing any other procurement criteria.

### 2.3.3 Control

There is some form of risk for everyone involved in a construction project. In this context, risk may be thought of as the possible loss resulting from the difference between what was anticipated and that which actually occurred. Risk need not be entirely monetary. It can involve time or quality. The results, however, are often translated into monetary terms. The amount of risk can be reduced, but it cannot be removed entirely. The chances of a building being constructed in a wholly satisfactory way are improved if an experienced contractor is selected.

In broad terms, control goes with risk. At one extreme of the procurement spectrum is the fixed price lump sum contract. In this, the contractor is shouldering most of the risk. He is gambling that the price he has quoted is sufficient to cover anything he has overlooked together with any inadequacies in his construction team. If the contract provisions are especially onerous, for example if the extension of time provisions covers only employer defaults and there are tough defects clauses, the contractor may be taking a real gamble on such things as the weather, labour relations, the skill of his men, the attitude of the clerk of works and the architect, until a point may be reached where the contractor is unwilling to tender at all because the risk is too great.

At the other end of the spectrum, the employer will take most of the risk if a management contract is used. It will operate on a cost reimbursement principle. The risk that the price will be greater than expected will fall squarely on the employer because the contractor will be entitled to be paid costs plus a management fee.

Getting the contractor to take a risk will cost the employer money. Although it may seem in the employer's best interests if the contractor can be made to take virtually all the risk of a contract, it must be remembered that the contractor will price the risk and if the risk does not materialise, the contractor gains extra profit. That is only fair and reasonable because risk management is or should be part of his skill for which the employer pays. If the employer is willing to take some risk, the result may be a very much cheaper project. By looking at the following contract provisions the allocation of risk can be assessed:

- Type of price.
- Contractor's obligations.
- Workmanship, materials and defects.
- Extensions of time.
- Payment.
- Loss and/or expense.
- Termination.

### 2.3.4 Quality

An employer who is seeking a high-quality building is looking for quality of design or of construction or, more commonly, both. Where design quality is paramount, an independent architect is clearly indicated. Where single-point responsibility is required, the employer has the option of:

**2.3    Key procurement criteria**

- Design and build.
- Design and manage.

In the former procurement system, the builder is responsible for driving the contract to completion, in the latter case it may be the architect who designs and co-ordinates the building work. In both instances there is the danger that the design may be constrained by:

- The capability of the constructor.
- Notions of profitability.

In the majority of cases, however, it is clear that designs emanating from either source achieve a high standard. Probably this is partly because architects will be involved in both systems and partly because design and buildability concerns will be married under one organisation.

Good-quality construction cannot really be separated from design, but a design may be mediocre in an aesthetic sense yet built of first class materials put together in a thoroughly sound way. It is doubtful whether a contractor-led procurement system will automatically result in a better quality of construction, but it probably will result in improved buildability. Certainly, it appears to be the case that involvement of the contractor early in the design process can have marked advantages in securing the most suitable constructional system which in turn should improve the quality of the construction.

Factors which will tend to work against the production of high quality construction are:

- Acceptance of the lowest tender.
- Short contract period.
- Complex work.
- Risk on the contractor.

Positive factors are:

- Sound design.
- Appropriate specification.
- Full, accurate and clear production information.
- Good supervision by the contractor.
- Proper inspection procedures by the architect.
- Competence, skill and experience of the contractor.
- Skills of operatives.
- Motivation of the contractor and his operatives.

### 2.3.5 Size/value

Size or value of a project alone is not a conclusive indication of the procurement or contract type most suitable. A relatively small building such as a clinic or laboratory may be so crammed with complex technology that it is a very expensive project, ideally suited to some kind of management or project management contract. A large simple building may be quite expensive, but suitable for a straightforward traditional procurement arrangement.

In considering the procurement criteria, therefore, size and value can be considered as giving an indication of the most appropriate procurement system or contract, but these criteria may not be the crucial factors in terms of decision making. Larger projects may need a further tier of management. On smaller schemes this may be too cumbersome.

### 2.3.6 Complexity

Complexity may result from:
- The employer's requirements.
- Innovative design.
- Special construction methods.
- Nature of the site.
- Complex phasing of site operations.

It will have an effect on:
- Time.
- Cost.
- Control.
- Quality.

The more complex the project, the more important it is to involve the contractor at an early stage and, therefore, some form of two-stage negotiated tender is probably essential for highly complex work. A very simple project, such as a garage, warehouse or other large enclosed space, is suitable for simple procurement systems such as traditional tendering or design and build. The employer has little control over the complexity of his requirements, but he can greatly reduce the complexity of the procurement as a whole by considering his design and phasing requirements.

**2.4 Priorities**

No procurement method or form of contract will satisfy every criterion entirely. It is therefore important to determine the employer's priorities, or to put it another way, to rate his criteria. This can be done in a variety of ways. The important thing is not to try to equate the ratings. For example the value of quality can never be compared directly against complexity or time. The method chosen in this book is to examine the criteria in order of importance and rate them accordingly. For example,

12 = first priority, 11 = second priority, etc. These ratings will be used when choosing procurement and contract in Chapter 7. The following is a checklist which the architect should use to assist in establishing the criteria ratings. It should be made clear to the employer that it is counterproductive to class everything as very important! The rating system will enable clashes to be identified immediately:

| Criteria | | Importance | |
|---|---|---|---|
| | Very | | Not |
| | 12 11 10 9 | 8 7 6 5 | 4 3 2 1 |

- Time
  -Economy
  -Certainty

- Cost
  -Economy
  -Certainty

- Control
  -Risk to employer
  -Risk to contractor

- Quality
  -Design
  -Construction

- Size/value
  -Medium–large
  -Small–medium

- Complexity
  -Complex
  -Simple

Criteria such as size or complexity, although necessary to take into account in the selection process, are not to any significant extent in the hands of the employer. Just because two criteria have the same priority rating does not necessarily mean that one of them must be changed. It is usually best to proceed on the

**2** Procurement criteria

first analysis, and it may be that the priorities are not mutually exclusive. If, during the selection process, it becomes clear that both criteria with the same priority rating cannot be satisfied to the same degree, it is time to ask the employer to make a decision by specifying the objectives more clearly. A client's objections may also change as the project develops: the demand for new offices in an area may rapidly increase, causing his development to become more time focused. Reappraisal is, therefore, necessary at different stages.

# 3 Contract procurement

29

**3.1
Introduction**

Every construction project requires some form of design work and the execution of construction operations on site. If a satisfactory result is to be obtained in a particular case, procedures must be adopted which will deal with the organisation and co-ordination required for the problems associated with that situation.

Traditionally, an employer who wished to have a building constructed would commission an architect to prepare drawings and, if the scheme was sufficiently large, a quantity surveyor might be employed to prepare bills of quantities on which the contractors tendering could prepare prices. The system has worked reasonably well in the past although it has received criticism. The construction industry continues to devise new procurement systems aimed at dealing with specific situations and problems more effectively than traditional systems.

Procurement methods can be categorised in various ways. The following is the principle of division adopted in this book:
- Traditional – Competitive.
  – Negotiated/two-stage.
- Project management – Competitive.
  – Negotiated/two-stage.
- Design and manage.
- Design and build.
- Management contracting.
- Construction management.

It is important to understand that procurement methods can be examined in other ways. The two most important are:
- By method of price determination.
- By method of contractor selection.

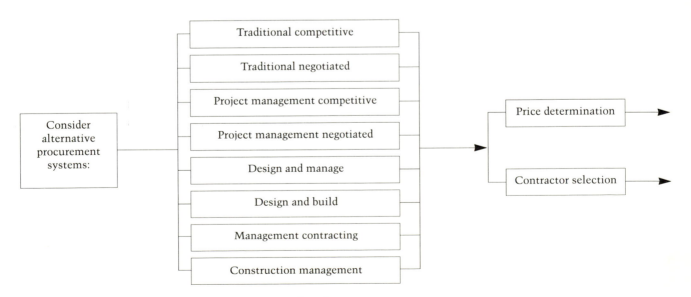

Deciding the procurement system.

Contractors are paid for the work they carry out on the basis of either:

- measurement; or
- cost reimbursement.

The differences were briefly discussed in section 1.5.3.

### 3.2.1 Measurement contracts

The main types of measurement contracts used in the construction industry are:

- Drawings and specification: The simplest type of measurement contract, only suitable for small or simple projects.
  – It can be difficult to interpret the tender information.
  – The contractor has to accept most of the pricing risk.
  – Contractors tend to overprice this kind of contract to compensate for possible errors or omissions.
  – If the project is too large, the fact that each contractor has to measure the quantities separately is wasteful of his resources and makes proper tender comparison difficult.
- Performance specification: The contractor has more freedom than when a traditional operational specification is used.
  – The contractor's price is based on the employer's brief and user requirements alone.
  – Within the parameters laid down, the contractor chooses the materials, construction and sometimes the design.
  – The contractor will naturally offer the least expensive materials and system of construction capable of satisfying the specification.
  – This type of specification is difficult to write properly.
  – Unless there are express terms to the contrary, the contractor generally undertakes that the finished building will be fit for its purpose if known and if there is no other designer involved.
- Schedule of rates: used where it is not possible to predetermine the nature and full extent of the proposed building works.
  – It is similar to a bill of quantities, although no quantities are included, but expected items are listed.
  – The principles of a Method of Measurement can be used and tenderers insert their own rates against the items. The rates are used to determine the successful tenderer and to calculate the final cost after remeasurement.
  – Neither the contract sum nor the probable final cost can be predicted.

**3  Contract procurement**

– It is difficult for contractors to price the schedules realistically in the absence of quantities.

- Schedule of prices: This is an alternative to the schedule of rates consisting of a schedule which is already priced when presented to the contractors. It is used extensively with measured term contracts. Tendering consists of the contractors adjusting each rate by adding or subtracting a stated percentage.

   – In practice, a single percentage adjustment is generally made to all the rates; this is unsatisfactory as the contractor will view the rates as varying between high and low.

   – A supposed advantage is that there are fewer errors in pricing when compared with the contractor's own price analysis of the work.

- Bills of quantities: Generally suitable for all but small projects.

   – Standardised qualitative and quantitative information enables tenders to be compared on price alone.

   – It is still the most common type of contract for major construction projects in the UK.

- Bills of approximate quantities: Used where it is not possible to measure the work accurately, but a reasonable idea of the work involved can be formed. Points:

   – The entire project is remeasured on completion.

   – A reliable forecast of the final cost is impossible, but an approximate cost can be obtained.

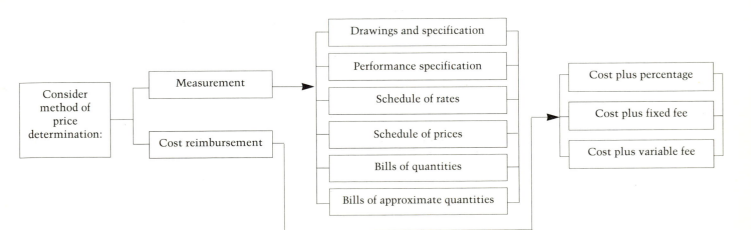

Deciding the method of price determination.

**3.2**  Methods of price determination

### 3.2.2 Cost reimbursement contracts

The main types of cost reimbursement contracts used in the construction industry are:

- Cost plus percentage: The contractor receives the cost of labour, materials, plant and sub-contractors (which need to be defined in the contract), to which is added a percentage to cover his overheads and profit.
  – A major disadvantage is that the greater the costs, the higher the fee because it is linked directly to the percentage. Therefore, there is no incentive to save money.
  – In practice, because of its simplicity, this system tends to be the selected method when using cost reimbursement.

- Cost plus fixed fee: The contractor receives his costs together with a fixed fee which roughly represents his overheads and profit. The fee is agreed before the commencement of the project.
  – In theory, the contractor receives the same fee no matter how much above or below the guide price the final account figure may be. There is therefore no direct incentive for the contractor to keep costs down.

**Table 3.1** Methods of price determination and forms of contract

| | JCT 80 With Quantities | JCT 80 With Approximate Quantities | JCT 80 Without Quantities | IFC 84 Intermediate Form | MW80 Minor Works Form | JCT 81 With Contractor's Design | JCT Fixed Fee Form | JCT 87 Management Contract | ACA 2 | ASI | ASI SW | ASI MW |
|---|---|---|---|---|---|---|---|---|---|---|---|---|
| Drawing and specification | – | – | ● | ● | ● | – | ● | – | ● | ● | ● | ● |
| Performance specification | – | – | – | – | – | ● | – | – | – | – | – | – |
| Schedule of rates | – | ● | – | ● | ● | – | – | – | ● | ● | ● | ● |
| Schedule of prices | – | ● | – | – | – | – | – | – | ● | ● | ● | ● |
| Bills of quantities | ● | – | – | ● | – | – | – | ● | ● | ● | ● | – |
| Bills of approximate quantities | – | ● | – | – | – | – | – | – | – | – | – | – |
| Contract sum analysis | – | – | ● | ● | – | ● | – | – | – | – | – | – |
| Cost plus contracts | – | – | – | – | – | – | ● | ● | – | – | – | – |

3   Contract procurement

- There is incentive for the contractor to maximise his profits by completing as quickly as possible and reducing costs.

- Because of the difficulty of predicting the final cost with sufficient accuracy, there may be disputes and, in practice, some provision to vary the fee is often included.

- Cost plus variable fee: A target cost is set before the contract is executed. The contractor receives his costs plus a fee. The fee is in two parts: a fixed amount and an amount which varies depending upon the extent to which the target cost is achieved.

  - The contractor has an incentive to keep costs as low as possible. How hard he tries will depend upon the scale of his reward. Complex sliding scales to determine the amount of the variable fee are sometimes employed.

  - A disadvantage is that the target cost has to be fixed on the basis of a very rough estimate of the proposed project.

Table 3.1 compares methods of price determination and forms of contract.

## 3.3 Contractor selection

Essentially, there are only two ways of choosing a contractor:

- competition; or
- negotiation.

The procedures were briefly discussed in section 1.5.2. The alternatives described later under Procurement options are used in conjunction with one of these methods of contractor selection.

### 3.3.1 Selective competition

In this system a number of firms of known reputation are selected by the design team to submit a price for the project. The firm submitting the lowest tender is normally awarded the contract. The National Joint Consultative Committee for Building has produced a Code of Procedure (1989) which provides useful guidance. The main points are:

- Maximum number of tenderers is six.
- The following should be considered when preparing a short list of tenderers:
  - The firm's financial standing and record.
  - Its recent experience of building over similar contract periods.
  - Its general experience and reputation for similar building types.

- – Adequacy of management.
- – Adequacy of capacity.
- The preliminary enquiry to determine willingness to tender should contain:
  - – Project title.
  - – Names of employer and consultants.
  - – Location of site and general description of the works.
  - – Approximate cost range.
  - – Principal nominated sub-contractors.
  - – Form of contract and amendments.
  - – Procedure for correction of priced bills.
  - – Whether contract under seal or under hand.
  - – Anticipated date for possession.
  - – Contract period.
  - – Anticipated date for despatch of tender documents.
  - – Tender period.
  - – Period tender must remain open for acceptance.
  - – Liquidated damages.
  - – Bond.
  - – Special conditions.
- Firms expressing willingness to tender should do so.
- Firms expressing willingness to tender and not chosen for short list should be notified immediately.
- Tenders must be submitted on the same basis:
  - – despatched on stated date.
  - – alternative offers based on alternative contract periods may be admitted only if so requested.
  - – standard forms of contract should not be amended.
  - – time of day should be stated for receipt of tenders and tenders received late should be returned unopened.
- Tender period should be not less than 20 working days.
- A qualified tender should be rejected if the tenderer refuses to withdraw the qualification without altering the tender figure.
- After tenders are opened, all but the lowest three should be informed that they are unsuccessful. The lowest should be asked to submit his priced bills or other document within four days. The next two should be told that they may be approached later.
- After acceptance, each tenderer should be given a full list of tender prices.
- The Code sets out alternative ways of dealing with errors in pricing.
- The employer is not bound to accept the lowest or any tender.

**3** Contract procurement

- The employer is not liable for tendering costs.
- The Code provisions should be qualified by the supplementary procedures specified in EC Directives which provide for a 'restrictive tendering procedure' in respect of public sector construction contracts above a specified value. Guidance is given in DOE Circular 59/73 (England and Wales) and SDD Circular 47/73 (Scotland).

This method of contractor selection is appropriate for almost any type of construction project where a suitable supply of contractors is available.

### 3.3.2 Open competition

Details of the project are advertised in the local press and contractors who feel that they are able to carry out the work are invited to submit their names for receipt of tender documents. Points:

- Advantage of introducing unknown firms to the design team.
- In theory any number of firms may submit a price.
- Very wasteful of the industry's resources, therefore, in practice, some selection takes place.
- No proper vetting takes place before tenders are submitted.
- Factors other than price must be considered when assessing the tenders.
- The lowest possible price will be obtained.
- The employer is not obliged to accept the lowest or any tender.
- The employer is not liable for tendering costs.

Sometimes open tendering is combined with selective tendering so that the procedure becomes:

- Advertisement placed inviting interested firms to submit names.
- Letter sent to all names received by set date. Letter requests details of firm, other contracts, referees and so on.
- Replies are vetted and the most suitable (maximum six) are selected to tender as in section 3.3.1 above.

This, however, is not true open tendering.

### 3.3.3 Negotiated contract

This method of contractor selection involves the agreement of a tender sum with a single contracting organisation. Negotiation is particularly suitable in the following circumstances:

- Where a business relationship exists between the employer and the building contractor.

**3.3**    Contractor selection

- Where, effectively, only one firm is capable of carrying out the work satisfactorily.
- If the contractor is already established on site carrying out another contract and 'continuation' is desired.

Advantages of negotiation are said to be:

- Fewer pricing errors because two parties are involved in the agreement of rates.
- Fewer claims from the contractor because competition is removed.
- Contractor participation in the design stage.
- Improved buildability.
- Early start on site.
- Greater co-operation between the contractor and the design team during the construction stage.

Disadvantages are said to be:

- Higher pricing than would be achieved by competition.
- If negotiations fail, the process must be started again from the beginning.
- A claims-minded contractor has the opportunity to work out a strategy based on perceived weaknesses.

Negotiation can be carried out in two ways:

- Negotiation with a single firm.
- Two-stage tendering.

If it is desired to negotiate with a single firm:

- The tender documents are prepared in the usual way.
- The contractor prices them.
- The quantity surveyor checks the prices.
- Contractor and quantity surveyor meet to settle queries and agree final rates.

If two-stage tendering (sometimes known as early selection) is desired:

- A simplified bill of quantities is prepared including the following sorts of items:
  – Site on-costs on a time-related basis.
  – Major items of measured works.
  – Specialist items, to allow the contractor the opportunity of pricing the profit and attendance sums.
- Tendering is carried out using selected contractors.
- During the first stage it is important to:
  – Provide a competitive basis for tender.
  – Establish the layout and design.
  – Provide clear pricing documents.
  – State the respective obligations and rights of the parties.
  – Determine a programme for the second stage.

**3   Contract procurement**

- A contractor is selected with whom further negotiation is carried out. The selection is on the basis of his rates for the items in the bills.
- During the second stage a proper tender is produced using the first-stage pricing of the bills as a basis for pricing bills of quantities prepared from the final design.

The National Joint Consultative Committee for Building has produced a Code of Procedure for two-stage tendering (1982). Many of the conditions outlined for single-stage tendering apply equally to two-stage tendering.

It should be noted that the public sector does not generally favour negotiated contracts because:

- Higher sums are involved and cost effectiveness must be demonstrated.
- Public accountability is more difficult to satisfy.
- Favouritism may be suggested.

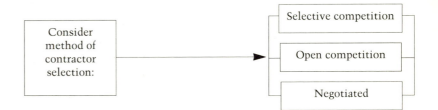

Deciding the method of contractor selection.

### 3.4 Procurement options

### 3.4.1 Traditional

Although this method of procurement should need little explanation, it is worth itemising the essential ingredients as follows:

- The employer appoints an independent architect to prepare designs based on the employer's brief, to produce constructional information, and to carry out administrative and inspection procedures during building works on site.
- If the project is sufficiently large, the employer appoints an independent quantity surveyor to prepare bills of quantities and to carry out valuation and cost advice functions throughout the execution of the project until final account stage.
- Depending upon the size and/or type of project, the employer appoints other consultants to assist in the design

and preparation of constructional information and to inspect the work in progress.

- When tender documentation is prepared, a contractor is selected by one of the methods outlined in section 3.3 above.
- The contractor's responsibility is to carry out the construction works strictly in accordance with the contract documents. He has no design responsibility and, generally, he may choose whatever methods he deems best to carry out the work.

Advantages can be:

- Independent design and professional advice for the employer.
- Widely recognised and used system of procurement.
- Possibility of flexible tendering arrangements.
- Good cost control.
- Certainty of standards before the contract is let.

**Fig. 3.1**
Traditional procurement.

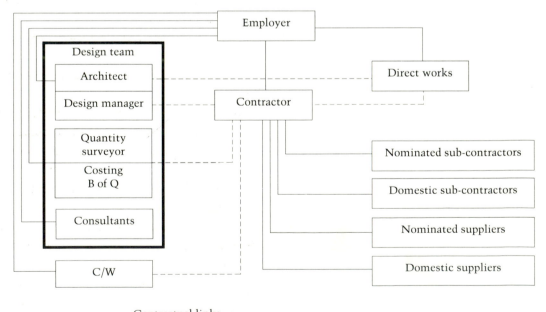

Contractual links ——————
Functional links  - - - - - -

3   Contract procurement

Disadvantages can be:
- Difficult to apportion liability if things go wrong.
- Difficult to involve contractor in the design process.
- Complex contractual relationships.
- Relatively long total period from inception to completion.
- Over-elaborate administration required, even for small projects.

The contractual relationships are shown in Fig. 3.1.

### 3.4.2 Project management

This is not a very precise term, but is generally (and taken in this book to be) the procurement system in which one person or organisation is appointed by the employer to deal with all matters concerning the project on the employer's behalf. It is sometimes termed Project Co-ordination. The project is management, rather than design, led. The project manager is responsible for appointing the consultants and the contractor, who all carry out their functions in a similar way to a traditional contract except that the administrative/management function is vested in the project manager. His functions include:

- Identifying the employer's requirements.
- Interpreting the requirements as necessary.
- Communicating the requirements to the design team.
- Programming, co-ordinating and monitoring all activities from the design to the construction stage.

Advantages can be:

- The management function can be put into the hands of a trained manager.
- The consultants are left to concentrate on their own specialities.
- It is more likely to result in a shorter project period.
- Overall control of time, cost and quality is more effective than when traditional methods are used, particularly when very large and/or complex projects are concerned.
- Flexibility of tendering arrangements.

Disadvantages can be:

- The employer pays for an additional professional who does no more than the design team would do anyway.
- The project manager acts simply as a postbox between employer and design team, worsening rather than improving communications.
- Although a professional manager appears to be the ideal project manager, in practice he must have a good

**3.4**    Procurement options

knowledge of construction techniques and, thus, expertise is duplicated.

- If the project manager is a constructional professional, disputes may arise within the design team.
- Often, he has no clearly defined role.
- He gives the contractor opportunities for claims.

Any person can become a project manager, provided he has a grasp of the construction industry. His personality is more important than his particular profession. His role must be carefully set out so that there is no overlapping of functions. *The British Property Federation (BPF) Manual* is the only document of its kind which sets out in detail the operation of a project management system. It is claimed that:

- It is flexible.
- It lacks the compromises inherent in agreements emanating from joint bodies such as the Joint Contracts Tribunal.
- It changes outdated attitudes.
- It alters the relationships between professionals.
- It creates better co-operation among members of the building team.

**Fig. 3.2**
Project management.

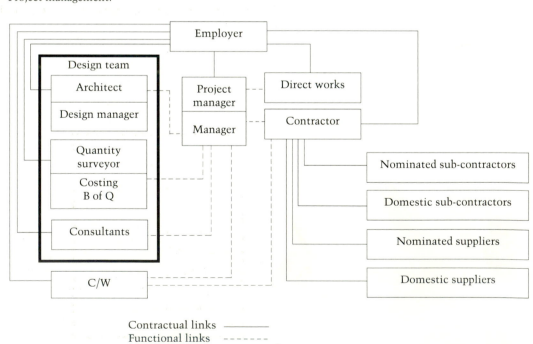

Contractual links ─────
Functional links ------

3   Contract procurement

- It aims to motivate.
- It reduces overlap of effort in the design team.
- It reduces the pre-tender period.
- It redefines risks.

The contractual relationships are shown in Fig. 3.2.

### 3.4.3 Design and manage

This is the consultant's counterpart to the contractor's design and build, but it is not yet as well established. It is sometimes referred to as Design Manage and Construct. The system may be led by an architect, engineer or surveyor to provide a total package for the employer. The professional effectively replaces the contractor in a role which at the present time is largely the management and co-ordination of sub-contractors.

Advantages can be:

- Single-point contractual responsibility.
- Suitable for all sizes and types of projects.
- Comparable with traditional methods in terms of cost and time.
- Quality control.

Disadvantages can be:

- Lack of independent professional advice.
- Difficult to obtain competitive tenders.
- Lack of experienced contractor input.

The contractual relationships are shown in Fig. 3.3.

**Fig. 3.3**
Design and manage.

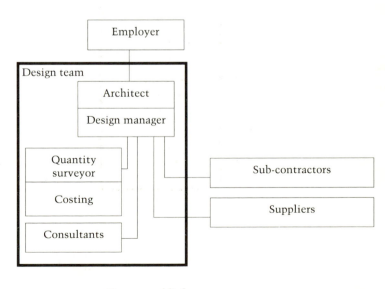

Contractual links ————

**3.4**   Procurement options

### 3.4.4 Design and build

The essence of this system is that the contractor is in control of both design and construction aspects of the project. He is the employer's point of contact in contrast with a traditional contract where the architect is the employer's contact. Although the design can be tackled by the contractor's in-house design team, if there is one, quite often the contractor will commission a firm of architects for that part of the work. In some instances, the firm may be nominated by the employer.

Many design and build schemes are carried out by one contractor who is selected on the basis of reputation. He produces a scheme and price from the employer's requirements and then proceeds with the project. Where competition is required, there may be problems. In view of the amount of work each tenderer is expected to do before finding out if his tender is successful, it is usual to keep the tender list low – no more than three contractors. The comparison of three different answers with the employer's requirements can be very difficult, especially if the best scheme has the highest price tag. In these circumstances, the employer needs an independent advisor to help him.

**Fig. 3.4**
Design and build.

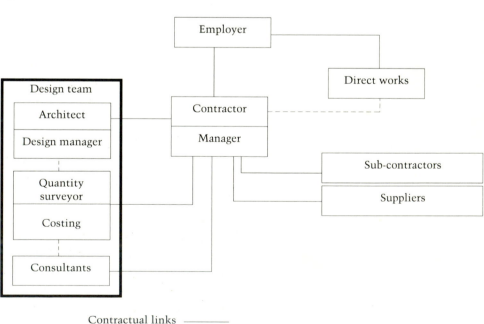

Contractual links ———
Functional links  - - - - - -

3   Contract procurement

In order to make comparison easier, the employer will sometimes engage an architect to produce an outline sketch and a detailed performance specification. The tenderers are left to develop the design in detail and to produce an operational specification. Comparison is still not easy and there are variations of the approach: for example, the contractors may be asked to produce a sketch scheme of their proposals together with a budget price. The most promising is chosen to develop the scheme and prepare a detailed price. Another method which is becoming popular involves the employer commissioning a design team to produce detailed designs. Tenders are invited on the basis that the chosen contractor will take on the design team as his own and will be responsible for the design. It is known as consultant switch.

Whatever the tendering arrangements are, the employer needs independent advice from architect, surveyor or engineer, or (ideally) both architect and quantity surveyor who can act as agent for the employer throughout all stages of the work. Advantages can be:

- Single point responsibility.
- Virtually guaranteed fixed cost and completion date.
- The contractor undertakes that the finished building will be fit for its purpose (unless JCT 81 is used when fitness for purpose will only apply to dwellings).
- Buildability of design concept.
- Fewer claims.

Disadvantages can be:

- Changes by the employer can be costly.
- The employer's requirements need care in preparation if the employer is to have them properly satisfied by the contractor's proposals.
- Design quality may suffer.
- The employer needs independent advice and thus is involved in additional fees, because the design fees will be included in the contractor's price.

The term package deal is often used to refer to design and build projects, but strictly the terms are not synonymous. A package deal refers to a design and build project which is chosen 'off the peg' from a catalogue. The employer will usually be able to view completed buildings of similar design and type. This type of procurement has been used extensively for the closed systems of industrialised buildings of timber or concrete. Multi-storey office blocks and flats, low-rise housing, workshop premises and farm buildings have been constructed on this basis.

**3.4** Procurement options

Advantages can be:
- Speed of erection.
- Fabrication under factory conditions results in high quality.

Disadvantages can be:
- Relatively little scope for change in basic design.
- Maintenance can be costly.

Another variation of design and build is the turnkey contract. In this system the contractor provides everything including furnishing and equipment from inception of the scheme to completion. All the employer has to do on completion is turn the key, hence the name. Some turnkey contracts require the contractor to find a suitable site for development and even to arrange long-term repair and maintenance. For this kind of system to work properly, the employer must provide a very precise and detailed brief and he must not make changes.

The contractual relationships are shown in Fig. 3.4.

### 3.4.5 Management contracting

This is a system in which the contractor is selected at an early stage and appointed to manage the construction process and input his own expertise during the pre-construction stage. For his services, the contractor receives a fee usually on a percentage basis (see section 3.2.2) which the parties agree before the contractor is appointed. If a fixed fee is agreed, there is usually some provision for adjustment if the actual cost varies more than a specified amount from the target cost.

The management contractor does not usually carry out any construction work himself. The work is divided into convenient packages which are put out to tender separately to sub-contractors. The management contractor may be selected on the basis of reputation or after tenders. Tendering is as much on management capability as anything else. Each tenderer has to state the percentage fee he requires, but it is seldom that there is a significant difference. Accurate cost planning and programming is essential for success. The system is most useful for large and complex contracts when considerable co-ordination of specialists is required and early completion is vital.

Advantages can be:
- An early start on site is possible.
- It is possible to achieve a short overall period from inception to completion by telescoping the pre-construction and construction stages.
- The overall lowest price should be achieved as a result of works package tenders.

- Details and changes can be incorporated up to a late stage in the construction stage.
- The contractor works as part of the design team.

Disadvantages can be:

- The final cost is not certain until the last works package tender has been received.
- The employer carries most of the risk.
- Everything depends on the skill of the management contractor.

The contractual relationships are shown in Fig. 3.5.

**Fig. 3.5**
Management contracting.

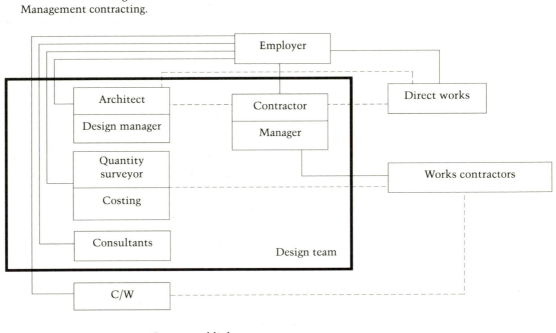

Contractual links ──────
Functional links ─ ─ ─ ─ ─

### 3.4.6 Construction management

This system has something of the flavour of project management and management contracting. The management contractor is appointed and paid a fee, and he is responsible for inviting works package tenders and managing and co-ordinating the works. Usually, the design team are separately appointed by the employer, but sometimes their appointment is left in the hands of the contractor. An important difference between this and the management contract is that the packages form a number of separate contracts with the employer. The system is little used in the UK.

**3.4**    Procurement options

Advantages can be:

- Contractor's expert input at design stage.
- Employer has complete control.
- Early start on site and short overall period to completion.
- Development of design can continue throughout the construction stage.
- It should result in the lowest cost.
- High quality should be achieved.

Disadvantages can be:

- The employer takes all the risk.
- No guarantee that the completion date will be achieved.
- The final cost is not certain until the last works package tender has been received.

The contractual relationships are shown in Fig. 3.6.

**Fig. 3.6**
Construction management.

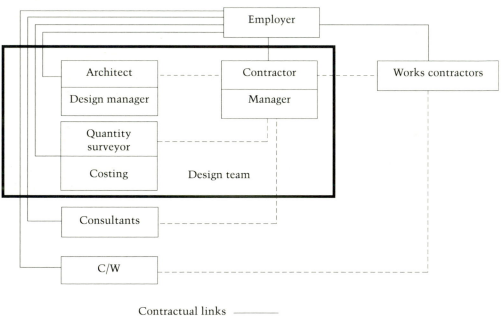

Contractual links ――――
Functional links  ― ― ― ―

# 4 Available forms of contract

**4.1**
**Introduction**

In order to choose the correct form of contract for any particular situation, it is essential, among other things, to be aware of the many forms available. A detailed knowledge of each form is also required. It is almost beyond the ability of one person to carry this kind of information in the head when one takes account of the multiplicity of forms and the number of apparently never-ending amendments. It is certainly beyond the ability of the practitioner who has a great many other things to think about at the same time. In the nature of things, you will be most familiar with the forms you have most recently dealt with.

This chapter provides what is hopefully an easy introduction to a selection of standard forms in common use. Although there is no doubt that the JCT series enjoys the greatest overall use (see Table 4.1), the possibility of using other forms should not be overlooked. The idea is to provide a summary of the main points of each form, the advantages and disadvantages and some advice on use. A quick reference to the advantages and disadvantages of each form is shown in Table 4.2. A word of warning, the authors do not necessarily recommend all the forms referred to in this chapter.

**Table 4.1**
Comparison of use of standard contract forms 1987

| Standard forms | % by value |
|---|---|
| JCT 80 With Quantities | 30.12 |
| JCT 80 With Approximate Quantities | 2.35 |
| JCT 80 Without Quantities | 9.69 |
| IFC 84 | 5.79 |
| MW 80 | 2.11 |
| JCT 81 | 8.67 |
| JCT Fixed Fee | 4.69 |
| ACA 2 | 0.21 |
| ASI | 0.09 |
| JCT 63 | 10.07 |
| Other forms | 26.21 |
| Total: | 100.00 |

Data extracted from the third JO (QS) survey – contracts in use 1987 published in *Chartered Quantity Surveyor*, January 1989.

**4.1**  Introduction

**Table 4.2**
Standard forms of contract

| Contract | Advantages | Disadvantages |
| --- | --- | --- |
| JCT 80 With Q | Comprehensive<br>Negotiated<br>Widely accepted<br>Range of ancillary<br>documents/special supplements | Complex clause numbering<br>Long<br>Complex nomination terms<br>Complex payment terms<br>Complex extension and loss and/or expense terms<br>Inflexible |
| JCT 80 With Approximate Q | As with Q version<br>Early start | As with Q version |
| JCT 80 Without Q | As with Q version | As with Q version |
| IFC 84 | Comprehensive<br>Negotiated<br>Becoming widely accepted<br>Flexible<br>Cross-referencing by subjects<br>Failure of work term<br>Range of ancillary documents | Not suitable for complex specialist work<br>Not suitable for long or complex projects<br>Complex naming terms<br>Not as simple as it looks |
| MW 80 | Negotiated<br>Widely accepted<br>Short<br>Easy to read<br>Flexible contract documents | Inadequate financial claims<br>No nominated sub-contractors<br>Inadequate insurance<br>No real fluctuations |
| JCT 81 | Negotiated<br>Comprehensive<br>Widely accepted<br>Single responsibility<br>May be faster than traditional contracts | Employer's requirements need careful preparation<br>Careful inspection<br>Employer may pay twice<br>Contractor has limited design liability<br>Contractor's proposals and employer's requirements may not correspond<br>Long<br>Poor clause numbering |
| Fixed Fee Prime Cost | Negotiated<br>Useful if extent not known | Difficult tendering<br>Final cost unknown<br>No change in fee<br>Similar problems to JCT 63 |
| JCT 87 Management | Negotiated<br>Comprehensive<br>Wide range of projects<br>Range of ancillary documents | High risk to employer<br>Complex form<br>Pre-construction procedure is unusual |
| ACA2 | Relatively simple<br>Flexible in use<br>Traditional or design build<br>Simple named sub-contractor provisions<br>Simple payment terms<br>Adjudication option<br>Built-in sectional completion<br>Clear responsibility divisions<br>Standard sub-contract | Not negotiated<br>Not widely accepted<br>High tenders<br>Unrealistic time periods<br>Some poor clause wording |

**4   Available forms of contract**

| Contract | Advantages | Disadvantages |
|---|---|---|
| ASI | Simple English<br>Good reputation<br>Relatively comprehensive<br>Sub-contract form | Poor layout<br>Not negotiated<br>Ambiguous clauses<br>Inadequate nominated sub-contract provisions |
| ASI SW | Simple English<br>Good reputation<br>Relatively comprehensive<br>Sub-contract form | Poor layout<br>Not negotiated<br>Ambiguous clauses<br>Inadequate nominated sub-contract provisions<br>Bad extension of time and loss and/or expense clauses<br>Arbitrator's powers not stated |
| ASI MW | Simple English<br>Good reputation<br>Relatively comprehensive | Poor layout<br>Not negotiated<br>Ambiguous clauses<br>Bad extension of time clause<br>No loss and/or expense clause<br>Little protection for employer<br>Arbitrator's powers not stated |

**Table 4.3**
Reasons why JCT 63 should
not be used

- Employer's 'written standard terms of business' and, therefore, caught by Section 3 of the Unfair Contract Terms Act 1977
- In the case of ambiguity, will be interpreted *contra proferentem*
- Fluctuations are not 'frozen' if contractor is in default as to time
- Poor extension of time provisions
- Poor loss and/or expense clause
- Inadequate nomination provisions
- No provision to defer possession of site
- No list of persons as sub-contractor provisions
- Unfair determination provisions
- Sequential working cannot be enforced
- Unclear position following insolvency of contractor

## 4.1 Introduction

**4.2**
**JCT 80 Standard Form of Building Contract With Quantities**

This is the standard form of contract from the JCT stable. It was introduced in 1980 in succession to JCT 63. It was very unpopular and JCT 63 continued to be used for a considerable period. JCT 63 is unfortunately (see Table 4.3) still in use in some places. JCT 80 was perceived as being longer and less comprehensible than its predecessor. Although some of the problem had more to do with familiarity than anything else, there was some truth in the observations.

There is no doubt that the form is complex and difficult to comprehend. That situation has not been improved by the mass of amendments which flow from JCT, the latest of which, Amendment 9, deals with VAT. JCT 80, however, has some significant advantages:

- It is comprehensive, being constantly updated to take account of legal decisions and covering most common and a few less common (Hostilities, Antiquities) situations.
- It is a negotiated document and therefore is unlikely to be caught by the provisions of the Unfair Contract Terms Act 1977. Section 3 of the Act provides for the situation where one party deals on the other's written standard terms of business. The other party may not exclude liability for breach by reference to any contract term nor claim to be entitled to do less than reasonably expected of him under the contract or to do nothing at all. Negotiated documents are not construed *contra proferentem* against the employer.
- It is the most widely used and accepted form in the building industry. Although it may not be understood, it is generally recognised.
- It has a range of documents which can be used with it:
  Nominated Sub-Contract Tender and Agreement NSC/1 and NSC/1a
  Employer/Nominated Sub-Contractor Agreement NSC/2 and NSC/2a
  Nomination of a Sub-Contractor NSC/3 and NSC/3a
  Nominated Sub-Contract NSC/4 and NSC/4a
  Tender for Nominated Supplier TNS/1
- It has special supplements to suit circumstances:
  Sectional Completion Supplement
  Contractor's Designed Portion Supplement.

There are also some disadvantages:
- An inhuman and readily forgettable system of clause numbering.
- Excessive length.
- Appallingly complex nomination provisions.

- Complex payment provisions.
- Over-elaborate extension of time and loss and/or expense provisions.

The form is available in local authority or private editions. The difference is generally one of detail. The form can be used for any value of contract and over any contract period. In practice, however, it is seldom used for contracts having a value of less than £200,000, because there are shorter alternatives which will suffice in most instances. It is especially suitable for traditional contracts of a complex nature or with complex service installations.

**4.3**
**JCT 80 With Approximate Quantities**

This is a variant of the standard form. Most of the comments included under that heading are equally applicable to this form. Its essential feature, as the name suggests, is bills of approximate quantities which define the quality, but only the approximate quantity of the works. The approximate quantities are used to provide a tender price and, more importantly, rates for the work which is all re-measured on completion.

The use of the form is similar to JCT 80 with quantities, in terms of size of contract and length of contract period. However in view of the relative price uncertainty its use is normally confined to situations where there is an urgency to proceed with the construction which will not allow the preparation of complete production information before bills are taken off. In considering whether to use this form, the advantages of early start (and presumably early finish) must be weighed against the lack of precise control over the final price.

**4.4**
**JCT 80 Without Quantities**

This is a variant of the standard form. It contains most of the characteristics of JCT 80 with quantities except, as the name suggests, bills of quantities. Instead, the contractor is expected to tender on the basis of drawings and either a specification or schedules of work. Practice Note 20 July 1988 revision, issued by the Joint Contracts Tribunal, advises that bills of quantities are probably necessary if the work has a contract value of more than £120,000, but this is only a guide. The value is not conclusive, however, and complex works of less value might indicate the use of bills of quantities while simple repetitive works of greater value might be suitable for this variant of the standard form.

**4.5
IFC 84 Intermediate Form of
Building Contract**

This form of contract which was introduced in 1984 was immediately popular. It bridges the gap between JCT 80 and MW 80. It appears much shorter than JCT 80, but in fact it is about two-thirds its length. Its apparent brevity owes a lot to the layout which is in two column format, and to the way the clauses are organised into only nine instead of 41 main sections.

Practice Note 20 recommends its use where the proposed works are:

- of a simple content involving the normally recognised basic trades and skills of the industry;
- without any building service installations of a complex nature, or other specialist work of a complex nature;
- adequately specified, or specified and billed, as appropriate prior to the invitation of tenders.

It is advised that the form would be most suitable for use, subject to the above criteria, when the contract period is not more than 12 months and the value is not more than £280,000 (at 1987 prices). Contract period and value are not the deciding factors. The Note contains a warning that the provisions of IFC 84 are less detailed than in JCT 80 and, if used for unsuitable works, circumstances may arise which could prejudice the equitable treatment of the parties. Some advantages of the form are:

- It is comprehensive, covering most situations which will arise if in less detail than JCT 80.
- It is a negotiated document and not likely to be caught by the Unfair Contract Terms Act 1977 or to be construed *contra proferentem* by the courts.
- It is becoming widely accepted for work where JCT 80 is not strictly necessary.
- It is flexible in use.
- The clauses cross reference by subject, not just by number.
- Provision for opening up and testing similar work to failed work.
- There is supporting documentation:
  Form of sub-contract tender NAM/T
  Employer/Specialist Agreement ESA/1
  Sub-contract NAM/SC

It has disadvantages:

- It is not suitable for complex specialist work.
- Not suitable for long or complex contracts.
- There are complex naming provisions.
- It is deceptively easy to understand compared with JCT 80.

**4**  Available forms of contract

The form is intended for private or local authority use and in the few instances which call for it, appropriate provisions are incorporated in the text. A wide range of supporting documents (specification, schedules of work, bills of quantities, drawings) may be used, but it is important that the design team have prepared a complete set of production information before tendering, because the essence of this contract is that disputes are avoided as much as possible. In practice, the form is increasing in popularity to the extent that it appears to be replacing JCT 80. The result is that IFC 84 is being used in circumstances which are sometimes inappropriate.

**4.6**
**MW 80 Agreement for Minor Building Works**

This is a very short form of contract even with the supplementary memorandum. For that reason alone it is popular. The current edition was produced in 1980. Practice Note M2 recommends the form is used:

1. When minor building works are to be carried out for an agreed lump sum and the employer has appointed an architect.

2. Where the lump sum offer has been obtained on the basis of drawings and/or specification and/or schedules but without detailed measurements. Therefore, the documents should enable the contractor to accurately identify the works without the need for bills of quantities.

3. Where the period for execution of the works is short enough not to warrant full labour and materials fluctuations.

4. Where the work is up to £70,000 in value (1987 prices).

5. Where the employer does not wish to nominate or use specialists.

   The value need only be taken as a rough guide. The important thing to remember is that this form is very basic in concept. Its principal use is for small houses and extensions. The advantages of the form are:

   • It is a negotiated document, therefore, it is not likely to be caught by the Unfair Contract Terms Act 1977 nor fall under the *contra proferentem* rule.

   • It is widely accepted in the building industry as a serviceable form for small works.

   • Short, easy to read and understand.

   • Within its range the contract documents are flexible. A contract can be executed with only the printed form and drawings, specifications, schedules of work or all three types of information.

The disadvantages are:

- No proper provision for financial claims. There is a very limited provision in clause 3.6 by virtue of Amendment MW5 issued in July 1988, but in general, the contractor can only claim loss and/or expense if he brings an action for damages at common law.
- No nominated sub-contractors. Many would consider this to be an advantage, but if specialist sub-contractors are required there is no provision for either direct appointment or nomination through the contract. There is nothing to prevent such specialists being named in the specification, but there is an absence of provisions to cover such things as termination and renomination.
- Brief and, in some circumstances, inadequate insurance provisions.
- No proper fluctuation provisions thus limiting use.

Many of the disadvantages can be overcome by the insertion of special clauses. To do this, however, would be to negate the main reason for using the form – its brevity. If it is considered necessary to add clauses, it makes more sense to consider the use of a more sophisticated form.

Although the form is easy to read and appears simple, it is deceptive. It is not designed to cope with complex projects. A number of legal actions have resulted from unsuitable use. It has been commonly used with bills of quantities although there are no provisions for them and it is clear that the employer does not warrant their correctness.

**4.7**
**JCT 81 With Contractor's Design**

Published in 1981, the details of this form are very similar to JCT 80. The essential difference is that JCT 81 is intended for use where the design and constructional information is to be provided by the contractor. There is no provision for an architect in the contract, but for an employer's agent who will presumably carry out certain administrative functions on behalf of the employer. In practice, of course, the agent might well be an architect, surveyor, engineer or perhaps a clerk of works. The employer will certainly also need specialist cost advice regarding payment.

The advantages of the form are:

- It is a negotiated document not likely to be caught by the Unfair Contract Terms Act 1977 nor by the *contra proferentem* rule.
- It is comprehensive.

**4**   Available forms of contract

- It is widely accepted, but, it must be said, widely abused in use. It is, for example, common for it to be used to contract sub-contractors directly employed through the agency of a project manager or a management contractor, quite irrespective of whether the sub-contractor in question has input any of the design content.
- Provides a single point of contact and responsibility to the employer for all aspects of the work.
- It may enable the building to be constructed faster than if independent professionals are used.

The disadvantages are:

- A long time must be spent in formulating the Employer's Requirements if the employer is to be certain of getting what he wants.
- The employer must set up careful inspection procedures in order to achieve quality.
- The employer may be in the position of paying two sets of professional fees: the 'hidden' design costs of the contractor and for the services of independent professionals to protect his interests.
- The contractor has limited design liability. Limited by total value and limited to the professional standard of care. If the contractor were to carry out a design and build contract on the basis of a simple exchange of letters it would doubtless have many problems, but the contractor's responsibility would be to produce a building fit for its purpose. The form, therefore, substantially reduces the contractor's normal implied liabilities.
- There may be difficulties in ensuring that the Contractor's Proposals cover all the employer's requirements. Any failures in this respect inevitably result in additional costs.
- Excessively long with a poor system of clause numbering.

It is perfectly possible for the employer to set out his requirements in a very brief document provided he accepts that the contractor will have maximum scope for interpretation. The employer should look at his requirements in the same way as he would prepare a brief for an architect. The contractor will often employ a consultant architect to carry out the design work, but it is important to remember that this architect will not be independent.

**4.8**
**Fixed Fee Form of**
**Prime Cost Contract**

This form bears many similarities to JCT 63. It was first issued in 1967 and last revised in 1976. It is intended for use where the works cannot be defined at tender stage. Thus it is particularly

**4.8**   Fixed Fee Form of Prime Cost Contract

suitable for alteration works. The contract documents are sparse. They consist of the printed form together with a specification and perhaps some drawings.

The whole basis of the contract is that the specification and drawings describe the work to the extent that it is known or assumed and the architect will have power to issue instructions for variations as the work progresses. There are, however, safeguards against the possibility of the architect issuing instructions which might, in total, change the nature and scope of the works.

The contractor prepares an estimate of the final cost and submits a fixed fee for carrying out the work. In addition, he is paid the actual cost of labour and materials necessary to do the work. The philosophy is clearly that, if the contractor gets the same fee whether he performs quickly or not, he will have an incentive to work quickly to try to maximise his profits. The contractor may be reluctant to tender for work if the extent is really unknown and variants of the fixed fee are sometimes used to relieve the situation. The principal alternative is a fee based on a percentage of the total cost coupled with a sliding deduction or addition insofar as the contractor meets a target cost. The advantages of this form are:

- Negotiated, therefore, it is not likely to be caught by the Unfair Contract Terms Act 1977 nor fall under the *contra proferentem* rule.
- Useful if the exact extent of the work is unknown.

The disadvantages are:

- It is difficult to obtain realistic competitive tenders due to the uncertainty of the work. The basis of the tender requires careful thought.
- The final cost of the work is unknown. The employer is, therefore, setting out on a voyage of discovery in that respect and it is important that he realises it. The alternative is for him to wait until full investigations have been completed so that full bills of quantities can be produced, but circumstances may prevent this.
- In its unamended version, the contractor receives the same fee no matter how efficient or inefficient he may be.
- The provisions, closely related to JCT 63, have similar deficiencies.

Unlike the management contract, this form envisages that the contractor will carry out part if not all of the work himself. His is not merely a management role.

**4**   Available forms of contract

**4.9**
**JCT 87 Management Contract**

This form of contract was issued in 1987 in response to the demand for a standard form of contract for this type of building procurement. It has some things in common with the fixed fee form and many of the clauses follow JCT 80 in approach.

The philosophy of this form is quite different from the traditional contract. The employer appoints a professional team who produce project drawings and specification. At this stage the contractor is introduced and works with the team although it should be noted that the form stops short of making the contractor part of the team. Indeed, at certain times, the contract distances the team from the contractor and forces them to assume traditional positions.

The contract is carefully divided into pre-construction and construction periods with the possibility of aborting the project in between. The management contractor does not actually carry out any work. His function is solely to organise and manage the work which is carried out by works contractors. He is paid on the basis of a fixed fee (with a possibility of adjustment) and the prime cost of all the work and materials in the works contract packages, together with anything he may do which is incidental to his management role.

Practice Note MC/1 sets out the criteria for using the form:

1. The employer wishes the design to be carried out by an independent architect and design team.
2. There is a need for early completion.
3. The project is fairly large.
4. The project requirements are complex.
5. The project entails, or might entail, changing the Employer's Requirements during the construction period.
6. The employer, while requiring early completion, wants the maximum possible competition in respect of the price for the building works. The advantages of using this form are:
   - It is a negotiated document and not likely to be caught by the Unfair Contract Terms Act 1977 nor to be construed *contra proferentem* by the courts.
   - It is comprehensive.
   - It can be used for a wide variety of projects.
   - It has a range of documents which can be used with it:
     Invitation to Tender, Tender and Articles of Agreement Works Contract/1;
     Works Contract Conditions Works Contract/2;
     Employer/Works Contractor Agreement Works Contract/3;
     Phased Completion Supplements for Management Contract and Works Contract.

The main disadvantages are:

- There is very little risk for the contractor, but correspondingly high risk for the employer.
- The form is complex and the implications are not easy to understand.
- The pre-construction contract procedures are unusual and could give rise to difficulties.

There is no upper limit on construction values or time periods. Under a certain value or complexity of project, there will be little point in entering into this form of contract. What that value or degree of complexity will be, depends on the type of project.

It is worth making the point that this form of contract depends entirely on the skill and experience of the management contractor. This in effect means the individual skills and experience of the managerial staff. Managerial skills of the high order vital to the successful outcome of this kind of contract are not common. Probably the most important part of the contractor selection process will be the consideration of the contractor's worth in this area. The fee part of any tender is likely to be similar if not identical among most contractors. It is in any case secondary to the considerations just mentioned, because they will decide whether the project finishes on time and to the contract cost plan, or late in a welter of variations and claims for financial reimbursement.

**4.10**
**ACA 2 Form of Building Agreement**

This form was first published in 1982 and a revised edition was issued in 1984. It is the result of consideration and consultation by the Association of Consultant Architects, who felt that a new form was needed which produced a better allocation of responsibilities and risk than JCT 80. There is another version available known as the British Property Federation Edition (BPF) whose principal difference is fewer optional clauses. That version is intended for use with the BPF system of building design and construction.

The form is intended to be flexible and remove the necessity for using a wide range of forms for different situations. It seeks to achieve this end by the inclusion of optional clauses. The advantages of this form are:

- Relatively simple and readily understandable.
- Flexible in use.
- Will suit traditional contracts or contractor design contracts.
- Simple named sub-contractor clauses.

- Simple payment clause.
- Adjudication option.
- There is 'built-in' provision for sectional completion.
- Clear division of responsibilities between employer and contractor.
- Standard sub-contract produced for use with the main form for named sub-contractors.

Disadvantages are:

- Not a negotiated form, therefore, it may be caught by the Unfair Contracts Act 1977 and be construed *contra proferentem* against the employer.
- It is not yet widely accepted. One difficulty appears to be that contractors consider the form to be weighted against them. This is incorrect, but the contract does allocate the risks clearly. In some cases these risks are given to the contractor when traditionally they might be considered to belong to the employer. This does not amount to unfair weighting because the contractor, clearly aware of his responsibilities, can plan accordingly.
- Tender costs might tend to be higher than when using other contracts because of the higher risk factor. The employer may accept that he pays more in return for less risk.
- The time periods allocated are not always realistic. It is not of great consequence provided the users remember to insert periods which are appropriate to the circumstances.
- Some of the clause wording is unsatisfactory.

The ACA form has a true acceleration clause. The architect is given power to accelerate and the contractor's consent is not required, although the architect is not to exercise his power unreasonably. It is also essential that the preparatory work is well organised before work commences because an important part of the contract is the time schedule which sets out, among other things, dates for the supply of information.

It will be used normally as a traditional contract (or in its slightly amended version with the BPF system) or to give the contractor major design responsibility after the architect has produced the initial design scheme. The contractor is required to take out design indemnity insurance.

**4.11 ASI Building Contract**

This contract was produced in 1986 by the Faculty of Architects and Surveyors as a complete revision of the 1975 edition. Although not used on a large scale the previous edition was very popular with its users and marked by very little serious dispute.

The 1986 edition, however, shows a complete change of format. In 1989 the Faculty of Architects and Surveyors merged with the Construction Surveyors Institute to become the Architects and Surveyors Institute.

The philosophy behind the form is that it is simple to understand and operate with an absence of legalistic English. It seems to be a praiseworthy objective, but overlooks the fact that many ordinary words do have precise legal meanings as a result of decided cases. The form is arranged in the usual way with recitals, articles, conditions and appendices. The conditions are arranged in ten sections. The advantages of the form are:

- Simple approach with generally understandable English.
- Good reputation.
- Relatively comprehensive.
- Sub-contract form available.

The disadvantages of the form are:

- Poor layout.
- It is not a negotiated form and it is therefore caught by the Unfair Contract Terms Act 1977 and would be construed *contra proferentem*.
- Many of the clauses are ambiguously worded.
- Totally inadequate nominated sub-contractor provision.

This is probably the kind of form which could be used if both parties already know and trust each other. It is intended for use on large projects, but one must doubt the wisdom of doing so in view of the ambiguous wording and inadequacy of some provisions.

**4.12**
**ASI Small Works Contract**

This form of contract is one of the set produced originally by the Faculty of Architects and Surveyors for use with smaller works such as a private house or alterations and extensions. It provides for nominated sub-contractors, but not for bills of quantities unless the supplementary conditions are incorporated which permit the engagement of a quantity surveyor and the use of bills of quantities. It is stated by the compilers not to be suitable for complex works.

It is similar in character and wording to the main ASI Building Contract and it has generally the same advantages and disadvantages. The advantages are:

- Simple approach with generally understandable English.
- Good reputation.
- Relatively comprehensive for the intended work.
- Sub-contract form available for nominated sub-contractors.

The disadvantages of this form are:
- Poor layout.
- It is not a negotiated form and, therefore, it would be caught by the Unfair Contract Terms Act 1977 and it would be construed *contra proferentem*.
- Some of the clauses are ambiguous.
- Totally inadequate nominated sub-contractor provisions.
- The extension of time and loss and/or expense clauses are seriously defective.
- Arbitrator is not given broad powers to open up and review decisions and so on.

If all parties know and trust each other and the work carried out under this form is of low value, say below £50,000, they may consider its use.

**4.13**
**ASI Minor Works Contract**

This is another form which originated from the Faculty of Architects and Surveyors. They recommend its use for minor works carried out on a lump sum basis with no nominated sub-contractors. It is not for use where bills of quantities are involved. It has many of the same advantages and disadvantages as the ASI Small Works Form. The advantages are:
- Simple approach with generally understandable English.
- Good reputation.
- Relatively comprehensive for the intended work.

The disadvantages are:
- Poor layout.
- Not a negotiated form and, therefore, it would be caught by the Unfair Contract Terms Act 1977 and it would also be construed *contra proferentem*.
- Ambiguous clauses.
- Seriously defective extension of time clause.
- No loss and/or expense clause.
- Arbitrator is not given broad powers to open up and review decisions.

This form is probably adequate if used purely for very low value works such as small extensions to domestic property. It must, however, be recognised that it does not protect the employer's position very well if a dispute should arise.

**4.14**
**JCT Contractor's Designed Portion**
**Supplement 1981**

This supplement is for use with JCT 80 With Quantities. It is not capable of use as a free-standing contract. It is for use when the works have been designed by an architect, but a portion of the works has been left to be designed by the contractor. The principle is that the supplement modifies JCT 80 only insofar as is applicable to the part designed by the contractor.

The supplement, therefore, closely follows JCT 81 to the extent of having Employer's Requirements, Contractor's Proposals and Analysis for that part of the works. There are some special provisions giving the architect responsibility for integrating the contractor's design with the rest of the works.

**4.15**
**JCT Sectional Completion**
**Supplement 1980**

This is the 1987 revision. The supplement is intended to adapt JCT 80 With Quantities for use where the works are to be completed in phased sections. The main adaptations involve the separation of the work into sections. A great many of the minor amendments are concerned to make clear that reference to the works also refers to any section.

There are separate dates for possession, completion, defects liability periods and liquidated damages for each section. There is, however, only one final certificate because there is only one contract. Failure to use the supplement where phasing is required can lead to grave difficulties and leave the employer open to claims from the contractor. If care is taken to make the appropriate amendments, the supplement may be used with JCT 80 With Approximate Quantities. There is a Sectional Completion Supplement for use with IFC 84 and a Phased Completion Supplement to the same effect for use when the JCT 87 Management Contract is used and the works packages are to be completed in phases or sections.

# 5 Selected contract terms

**Table 3.1**

Comparison of contract clauses

| Topics | JCT 80 With Quantities | JCT 80 With Approximate Quantities | JCT 80 Without Quantities | IFC 84 Intermediate Form | MW80 Minor Works Form | JCT 81 With Contractor's Design | JCT Fixed Fee Form | JCT 87 Management Contract | ACA 2 | ASI | ASI SW | ASI MW |
|---|---|---|---|---|---|---|---|---|---|---|---|---|
| Architect/contract administrator/advisor | ● | ● | ● | ● | ● | – | ● | ● | ● | ● | ● | ● |
| Quantity surveyor | ● | ● | ● | ● | ● | – | ● | ● | ● | ● | ● | – |
| Consultants | – | – | – | – | – | – | – | ● | – | – | – | – |
| Clerk of works | ● | ● | ● | ● | – | – | ● | ● | – | ● | – | – |
| Contractor's obligations | ● | ● | ● | ● | ● | ● | ● | ● | ● | ● | ● | ● |
| Discrepancies | ● | ● | ● | ● | ● | ● | ● | ● | ● | ● | ● | – |
| Statutory requirements | ● | ● | ● | ● | ● | ● | ● | ● | ● | ● | ● | ● |
| Information from architect | ● | ● | ● | ● | ● | – | ● | ● | ● | ● | ● | ● |
| Information from contractor | – | – | – | – | – | ● | – | ● | ● | – | – | – |
| Ground conditions | – | – | – | – | – | – | – | ● | – | – | – | – |
| Access by architect | ● | ● | ● | – | – | ● | ● | ● | – | – | – | – |
| Vesting of property | ● | ● | ● | ● | – | ● | ● | ● | ● | ● | ● | – |
| Insurance against injury to persons and property | ● | ● | ● | ● | ● | ● | ● | ● | ● | ● | ● | ● |
| Insurance of the works | ● | ● | ● | ● | ● | ● | ● | ● | ● | ● | ● | ● |
| Insurance against non-negligent damage to the works | ● | ● | ● | ● | – | ● | ● | ● | ● | ● | ● | ● |
| Insurance against loss of liquidated damages | ● | ● | ● | ● | – | ● | – | ● | – | – | – | – |
| Design indemnity insurance by contractor | – | – | – | – | – | – | – | – | ● | – | – | – |
| Loss and/or expense | ● | ● | ● | ● | – | ● | ● | ● | ● | ● | ● | – |
| Instructions | ● | ● | ● | ● | ● | ● | ● | ● | ● | ● | ● | ● |
| Valuation of variations | ● | ● | ● | ● | ● | ● | – | ● | ● | ● | ● | ● |
| Assignment | ● | ● | ● | ● | ● | ● | ● | ● | ● | ● | ● | ● |
| Sub-letting | ● | ● | ● | ● | ● | ● | ● | ● | ● | ● | ● | ● |
| Named sub-contractors | – | – | – | ● | – | – | – | – | ● | – | – | – |
| Nominated sub-contractors | ● | ● | ● | – | – | ● | – | – | ● | ● | ● | – |
| Employer's licensees | ● | ● | ● | ● | – | ● | ● | ● | ● | ● | ● | – |
| Liquidated damages | ● | ● | ● | ● | ● | ● | ● | ● | ● | ● | ● | ● |
| Unliquidated damages | – | – | – | – | – | – | – | – | ● | – | – | – |
| Extension of time | ● | ● | ● | ● | ● | ● | ● | ● | ● | ● | ● | ● |
| Extension of time review | ● | ● | ● | ● | – | ● | – | – | ● | – | – | – |
| Acceleration | – | – | – | – | – | – | – | ● | ● | – | – | – |
| Postponement | ● | ● | ● | ● | – | ● | ● | ● | ● | ● | – | – |
| Deferment of possession | ● | ● | ● | ● | – | – | – | – | ● | – | – | – |
| Practical completion | ● | ● | ● | ● | ● | ● | ● | ● | ● | ● | ● | ● |
| Defects liability period | ● | ● | ● | ● | ● | ● | ● | ● | ● | ● | ● | ● |
| Partial possession | ● | ● | ● | – | ● | ● | ● | ● | ● | ● | – | – |
| Payment | ● | ● | ● | ● | ● | ● | ● | ● | ● | ● | ● | ● |
| Fluctuations | ● | ● | ● | ● | – | ● | – | – | ● | ● | ● | – |
| Termination by employer | ● | ● | ● | ● | ● | ● | ● | ● | ● | ● | ● | ● |
| Termination by contractor | ● | ● | ● | ● | ● | ● | ● | ● | ● | ● | ● | ● |
| Termination by either party | ● | ● | ● | ● | – | ● | – | ● | ● | – | – | – |
| Antiquities | ● | ● | ● | – | – | ● | ● | ● | ● | ● | – | – |
| Hostilities | ● | ● | ● | – | – | ● | ● | ● | – | ● | ● | – |
| Adjudication | – | – | – | – | – | ● | – | – | ● | – | – | – |
| Arbitration | ● | ● | ● | ● | ● | ● | ● | ● | ● | ● | ● | ● |
| Litigation | – | – | – | – | – | – | – | – | ● | – | – | – |

**5.1**
**Introduction**
The idea of this chapter is to provide you with information about a wide variety of forms. Ultimately, you will make the decision which form to use. Any summary is achieved by cutting out much of the original material. After using the contents of this chapter to 'home in' on what appears to be a suitable form, you should take care to read the original form in order to absorb the full import together with any subtleties.

Every form in this chapter has been analysed in accordance with a format to make comparison easier (although detailed comparison of key clauses is carried out in Chapter 6). Where the analysis is the same, for example in some of the clauses in the many variations of JCT 80, cross referencing has been carried out. This highlights the essential differences between the variants of similar forms. See also Table 5.1. The headings used in the analysis are as follows:

i) Type of contract.
ii) The contract documents.
iii) Type of price.
iv) Provision for architect, etc.
v) Unusual provisions.
vi) Contractor's obligations.
vii) Provision of information.
viii) Statutory requirements.
ix) Site personnel.
x) Vesting of property.
xi) Insurance.
xii) Possession of site.
xiii) Completion, defects liability.
xiv) Extensions of time, damages for delay.
xv) Partial completion.
xvi) Assignment and sub-letting.
xvii) Employer's licensees.
xviii) Instructions.
xix) Payment.
xx) Variations and their valuation.
xxi) Loss and/or expense.
xxii) Contract sum.
xxiii) Antiquities.
xxiv) War.
xxv) Termination.
xxvi) Disputes.

**5.2**
**JCT 80 With Quantities**

i) Type of contract
This is a traditional form of contract dealing with the situation where the architect prepares the production information, the quantity surveyor prepares the bills of quantities, and the contractor tenders to carry out the work without any design responsibility. Ideally, the architect should be working to a very tight brief where the entire scope and nature of the work is known, although there is provision for variations in the work after commencement on site.

ii) The contract documents
- contract drawings; and
- contract bills; and
- printed form.

iii) Type of price
Lump sum. In principle, this is a fixed price contract although the contract provisions soften this effect as far as the contractor is concerned, for example, by providing for fluctuations to varying degrees and the valuation of variations.

iv) Provision for architect, etc.
Articles 3A and 3B provide for the insertion of the name of the architect or the contract administrator respectively. The Architects Registration Acts 1931 to 1969 make it an offence for any unregistered person to carry on business under the style 'architect'. The alternative article is for the use of unregistered persons. Article 4 provides for the insertion of the quantity surveyor's name. If any nominated person ceases to act, the employer must nominate some other person to whom the contractor does not object.

v) Unusual provisions
None.

vi) Contractor's obligations
Principally contained in clause 2.1 to carry out and complete the works in accordance with the contract documents. There is a proviso to the effect that if the approval of the quality of materials or the standard of workmanship is to be left to the architect, he must exercise his satisfaction reasonably. The final

**5** Selected contract terms

certificate is conclusive evidence that, where the architect has left such matters for his satisfaction, he is so satisfied.

vii) Provision of information

The architect must provide the contractor with a copy of the contract documents, two copies of the contract drawings and the unpriced bills of quantities and, as may be necessary, from time to time with further drawings or details sufficient to enable the contractor to carry out and complete the works in accordance with the contract. By optional clause 5.3.1.2, the contractor must provide the architect with two copies of his master programme and update it within 14 days of any extension of time decision.

Clause 2.2.1 provides that nothing in the bills of quantities can override or modify the printed form. The bills are to be prepared according to the Standard Method of Measurement of Building Works 7th Edition and errors in description or quantity are to be corrected and treated as variations under clause 13.2. The contractor has no duty to look for discrepancies between documents, but if he finds any, he must report them to the architect for his instructions. Clause 5.7 prohibits the contractor from using the documents except in connection with the works and neither employer, architect nor quantity surveyor must divulge the rates in the contract bills.

viii) Statutory requirements

The contractor must comply with and give all notices required by statute, and so on. Divergences, if found, must be reported to the architect for his instructions. Provided that this is done, the contractor has no liability to the employer if the works do not comply with statutory requirements. The contractor may carry out necessary work to comply with statutory requirements in an emergency, provided that he immediately reports the matter and the steps being taken to the architect as soon as he can reasonably do so.

ix) Site personnel

Clause 10 stipulates that the contractor must constantly keep a competent person-in-charge on the works. The architect is empowered by clause 8.5 to issue instructions requiring the contractor to exclude any employees from the works. The employer is entitled to employ a clerk of works who is under the direction of the architect and who may issue directions which have no effect unless confirmed by the architect. His function is solely that of an inspector.

**5.2**  JCT 80 With Quantities

x) Vesting of property
Clause 16 sets out the rules. Unfixed materials delivered to site may not be removed except with the architect's written consent. If the value is included in an interim certificate paid by the employer, he thereupon becomes the owner. Whether such a term will be effective depends upon the extent to which it is echoed in sub-contracts, sub-sub-contracts and contracts of sale. Similar rules apply to materials stored off-site.

xi) Insurance
Clause 20 provides for the contractor to indemnify the employer and take out insurance against personal injury or death, except to the extent that it is due to the employer's negligence, and against damage to property (except the works) to the extent that it is due to the contractor's negligence.

Provision is made in clause 21.2.1 for insurance to be taken out by the contractor (if the appendix states it may be required and the architect so instructs) in respect of employer's losses because of damage to property other than the works where negligence is not involved.

Clause 22 provides for insurance of the works. There are two categories of insurance:
- All risks; and
- Specified perils.

Specified perils includes the usual fire, lightning, explosion, storm, tempest, etc. All risks covers those and the additional risks of impact, subsidence, theft and vandalism.

Clause 22A applies to insurance of new works where the insurance is to be taken out by the contractor.

Clause 22B applies to insurance of new work where the insurance is to be taken out by the employer.

Clause 22C applies to works of alteration or extension to existing building where the insurance is to be taken out by the employer in regard to the existing and new part of the works.

All works insurance is to be in joint names against all risks except for insurance of existing buildings and contents which are to be in joint names against specified perils. There are provisions in respect of the production of evidence of insurance and power to insure by the other party in case of default. The contractor is obliged to restore damaged work in every case, but there are important provisos:
- If the contractor insures new work, he receives in payment, via the employer by certificates, only the amounts paid by

**5** Selected contract terms

the insurers. Thus he has to stand the amount of any excess or under-insurance.

- If the employer insures new work, the contractor is entitled to receive proper payment as though the restoration is a variation. The employer has to stand the amount of any excess or under-insurance.
- The situation is similar under clause 22C, but either party may determine the contractor's employment if it is just and equitable so to do.

Clause 22D provides (if it is stated in the appendix that the employer may so require) for insurance to be taken out by the contractor to provide payment to the employer of the amount of liquidated damages otherwise lost as a result of the architect granting the contractor an extension of time due to damage caused by a specified peril.

xii) Possession of site

Possession of the site is dealt with by clause 23. The employer must give possession on the date stated in the contract. The contractor must begin the works and proceed regularly and diligently to completion. The employer may not take possession of any part of the works until practical completion, but if the contractor consents the employer may use the site for storage or other purposes subject to confirmation that the insurance cover will not be prejudiced. The employer may defer giving possession of the site, if the Appendix states the clause 23.1.2 applies, for no more than 6 weeks.

xiii) Completion, defects liability

Clause 23.1 makes clear that the contractor must complete the works on or before the contract completion date. When the architect is of the opinion that the works have achieved practical completion, clause 17.1 stipulates that he must issue a certificate to that effect. Among other things, the defects liability period then starts and, when it is ended, the architect must send the contractor a schedule of defects within 14 days. After rectification of the defects, the architect issues a certificate of making good defects which signals the release of the second half of the retention money.

xiv) Extensions of time, damages for delay

The contractor must notify the architect whenever the works are or are likely to be delayed including the cause of the delay and any relevant event. As soon as possible afterwards, the

**5.2**   JCT 80 With Quantities

contractor must provide particulars and an estimate of the effect upon the completion date in respect of every relevant event. The architect's duty is to grant a fair and reasonable extension of time within 12 weeks or before completion date whichever is the nearer in time. After the first exercise of his duty, he may reduce extensions by taking omissions of the work into account. He must also review the extensions after completion date, but no later than 12 weeks after practical completion of the works. The relevant events may be summarised as follows:

- *Force majeure.*
- Exceptionally adverse weather.
- Damage due to specified perils.
- Civil commotion, strikes, etc.
- Compliance with architect's instructions.
- Late information.
- Delay by nominated sub-contractors.
- Employer's men or materials.
- Exercise of statutory power.
- Inability to obtain labour or materials.
- Statutory undertakers.
- Failure to give access.
- Deferment of possession.
- If approximate quantity not reasonably accurate.

If the contractor fails to complete the works by the contract or extended completion date, the architect must issue a certificate to that effect and the employer may then give notice and deduct liquidated damages at the rate stated in the Appendix.

xv) Partial completion

Clause 18 allows the employer to take possession of part of the works with the contractor's consent. The architect must give a written statement identifying the part and giving the date taken into possession. In respect of the part, various consequences follow very much as though the part had achieved practical completion and the appropriate certificate had been issued.

xvi) Assignment and sub-letting

Neither party may assign the contract, but the employer may assign to any future purchaser or lessee the right to bring proceedings if the Appendix so states.

Clause 19.2 allows the contractor to sub-let work with the architect's consent.

Clause 19.3 provides for the contractor to use a sub-contractor from a list of at least three inserted in the bills of quantities by the employer.

Clause 35 allows the employer to nominate a sub-contractor. It can arise in any one of eight ways, but usually it takes place as a result of a complex tendering process. There is provision for the contractor to object to the nominee and a series of complex provisions dealing with:

- Payment: the contractor is to be directed and there is provision for direct payment if the contractor defaults.
- Extension of sub-contract time and certification of failure to complete.
- Practical completion.
- Final payment: the procedure for rectifying sub-contract defects makes the contractor finally liable for any extra costs in rectifying defects.
- Contractor not liable for nominated sub-contractor's design.
- Position if renomination is necessary because the contractor reasonably objects, the proposed sub-contractor fails to settle details or enter into sub-contract, the sub-contractor abandons the work or his employment is determined.

xvii) Employer's licensees

Clause 29 provides that the employer may engage other contractors to work on the site in two circumstances:

- Where the work is noted in the bills of quantities; or
- Where the work is not noted in the bills of quantities but the main contractor has agreed.

In both instances there may be entitlements to extension of time and loss and/or expense.

xviii) Instructions

Under the provisions of clause 4, the architect may issue any instructions empowered by the contract. Unless it concerns a variation of sequence or hours of work etc., the contractor must carry out the work forthwith. The architect may issue a 7 day compliance notice and the employer may engage others. If the contractor questions the empowering clause, it is deemed valid if he thereafter complies. Oral instructions must be confirmed by the contractor or the architect.

xix) Payment

Complex provisions governed by clause 30. Certificates must be issued in accordance with time period in Appendix (normally 1 month) until practical completion. Payment must be made by

**5.2    JCT 80 With Quantities**

the employer within 14 days of a certificate issued by the architect. The value of work in a certificate must be as at a date no earlier than 7 days before certification. In the private edition, retention money must be deposited in a special bank account. Retention must be released, half at practical completion and half at certification of making good defects. There is a tight schedule for issue of the final certificate. Within 6 months after practical completion the contractor must submit all documents for the final adjustment of the contract sum. Ascertainment of loss and/or expense and statement of all adjustments must take place not more than 3 months after. The final certificate must be issued no more than 2 months after the latest of:

- Completion of making good defects.
- End of the defects liability period.
- Date ascertainment and statement sent to the contractor.

The final certificate is conclusive evidence, unless either party commences arbitration or other proceedings within 28 days of its issue, that:

- Quality and standards specified to be to architect's satisfaction are to his satisfaction.
- Contractual provisions requiring adjustment of the contract sum have been carried out.
- Extensions of time have been properly given.
- Loss and/or expense is in final settlement of all contractor's claims on clause 26 matters.

Fluctuations are the subject of optional clauses 38, 39 or 40 which allow fluctuations for contribution, levy and tax, labour and materials cost or the use of price adjustment formula respectively.

xx) Variations and their valuation

Variations are defined and rules set out for their valuation in clause 13. The basis of valuation is the rates in the bills of quantities or pro-rata, unless not appropriate when a fair valuation must be made or a daywork basis may be used. Omitted work is generally valued at bill of quantity rates. The valuation must be carried out by the quantity surveyor.

xxi) Loss and/or expense

The contractor may claim direct loss and/or expense if the date for possession has been deferred or if regular progress has been or is likely to be substantially affected due to any of the following matters:

- Late information.
- Opening up and testing.

**5**   Selected contract terms

- Discrepancies between documents.
- Employer's men or materials.
- Postponement.
- Failure to give access.
- Compliance with architect's instructions.
- Approximate quantity not a reasonably accurate forecast.

The contractor must make written application as soon as it is apparent that regular progress is or is likely to be affected, he must supply, on request, information to enable the architect to form an opinion, and he must supply, on request, details to enable ascertainment to take place. The contractor must also forward any application made by a nominated sub-contractor.

xxii) Contract sum

The quality and quantity of work is deemed to be that set out in the bills of quantities.

Clause 3 stipulates that where adjustments are to be made to the contract sum, the amounts must be included in the next interim certificate after ascertainment takes place. Adjustment is authorised in 23 different places in the conditions.

xxiii) Antiquities

Clause 34 deals with antiquities found on the site and provides that the contractor must notify the architect forthwith, doing everything feasible to preserve the object from harm. The architect must issue instructions and the contractor is entitled to loss and/or expense and extension of time as appropriate.

xxiv) War

Either party may determine the contractor's employment 28 days after general mobilisation of the armed forces and the architect may give instructions about protective work.

xxv) Termination

Either party may determine the contractor's employment for stipulated reasons:

The employer, after written notice, if the contractor:
- wholly suspends work without reasonable cause; or
- fails to proceed regularly and diligently; or
- does not comply with notice to remove defective work and as a result the works are substantially affected; or
- fails to comply with clause 19.

In the case of insolvency, determination is automatic.

**5.2**   JCT 80 With Quantities

The contractor if:

- the employer does not pay amount due after notice; or
- the employer interferes with a certificate; or
- the work is suspended for the period noted in the Appendix due to:
  - Architect's instructions; or
  - Late information; or
  - Employer's men or materials; or
  - Employer's failure to give access; or
  - Opening up of work.
- the employer is insolvent.

Either party if the works are suspended for a period noted in the Appendix due to:

- *force majeure*; or
- loss or damage due to specified perils; or
- civil commotion.

The provisions are to be found in clauses 27, 28 and 28A. The consequences of determination involve:

If the employer determines:

- He may pay others to complete the work.
- He may require the contractor to assign his rights in contracts with sub-contractors or suppliers.
- He may use contractor's plant and/or require its removal.
- He may charge the contractor loss and/or expense and the difference in cost of having others to complete. He must value work done, but need not pay the contractor until the work is completed and accounts drawn up.

If the contractor determines:

- He must remove his plant from site;
- He must be paid costs of removal together with value of work carried out and any loss and/or expense.

If either party determines under clause 28A, the situation is the same as if the contractor determines under clause 28 except that he cannot claim any loss or expense.

xxvi) Disputes

The procedure for dealing with disputes is to be arbitration. Article 5 and clause 41 apply. Either party may require a dispute to be referred by giving written notice to the other. If there is no agreement on the arbitrator, the President or Vice-President of either the RIBA, RICS or the CIArb can be asked to nominate. If there is a related arbitration involving a sub-contractor or supplier, the two references can be joined. It is stipulated that the parties agree that questions of law are to be determined by the High Court. The arbitrator has wide powers to order rectification of the contract and open up any certificate or decision of the architect. Except by agreement, arbitration cannot be opened until after practical completion, termination or abandonment of the work except in specified instances. Arbitrations are to be carried out under the JCT Arbitration Rules 1987 which provide for strict control of the type and timing of the procedures.

## 5.3
## JCT 80
## With Approximate Quantities

i) Type of contract
As section 5.2 except that it is likely that the extent of the work will not be known at tender stage.

ii) The contract documents
As section 5.2.

iii) Type of price
Complete remeasurement of work to convert the tender sum (the total of the approximate bills of quantities) into the ascertained final sum.

iv) Provision for architect, etc.
As section 5.2.

v) Unusual provisions
None.

vi) Contractor's obligations
As section 5.2.

vii) Provision of information
As section 5.2.

viii) Statutory requirements
As section 5.2.

ix) Site personnel
As section 5.2.

x) Vesting of property
As section 5.2.

xi) Insurance
As section 5.2.

xii) Possession of site
As section 5.2.

xiii) Completion, defects liability
As section 5.2.

xiv) Extensions of time, damages for delay
As section 5.2.

xv) Partial completion
As section 5.2.

xvi) Assignment and sub-letting
As section 5.2.

xvii) Employer's licensees
As section 5.2.

xviii) Instructions
As section 5.2.

xix) Payment
As section 5.2 except that the adjusted contract sum is known as the ascertained final sum and the fluctuations are limited to clauses 39 or 40 which allow fluctuations for labour and materials cost or the use of price adjustment formula respectively.

xx) Variations and their valuation
Variations are defined and the rules set out for their valuation in clause 14. All variations instructed by the architect and all work carried out is to be valued by the quantity surveyor. The basis of valuation is the rates in the bills of quantities or pro-rata unless they are not appropriate when a fair valuation must be made or a daywork basis may be used. Omitted work is generally valued at bill of quantity rates.

xxi) Loss and/or expense
As section 5.2.

**5** Selected contract terms

xxii) Contract sum
As section 5.2.

xxiii) Antiquities
As section 5.2.

xxiv) War
As section 5.2.

xxv) Termination
As section 5.2.

xxvi) Disputes
As section 5.2.


## 5.4
## JCT 80 Without Quantities

i) Type of contract
Similar to section 5.2, but the quantity surveyor is not involved
in producing bills of quantities; the architect prepares
production information together with a specification or
schedules of work.

ii) The contract documents
 • contract drawings; and
 • printed form; and
 • schedule to which rule 11b of the Formula Rules refers
   (where clause 40 is applicable); and either
 • Priced specification/Priced schedules of work, or
 • Unpriced specification. (The contractor must supply either
   a contract sum analysis or a schedule of rates, neither of
   which is a contract document.)

iii) Type of price
As section 5.2.

iv) Provisions for architect, etc.
As section 5.2.

v) Unusual provisions
None.

vi)  **Contractor's obligations**
As section 5.2.

vii)  **Provision of information**
The architect must provide the contractor with a copy of the contract documents, two copies of the contract drawings and the unpriced specification or schedules of work. Also as may be necessary, from time to time the architect must provide further drawings or details sufficient to enable the contractor to carry out and complete the works in accordance with the contract. From optional clause 5.3.1.2, the contractor must provide the architect with two copies of his master programme and update it within 14 days of any extension of time decision. Clause 2.2.1 provides that nothing in the specification/schedules of work can override or modify the printed form. Errors or inconsistencies in or between the contract drawings and specification/schedules of work are to be corrected and treated as variations to be valued under clause 13.4. The contractor has no duty to look for discrepancies between documents, but if he finds any, he must report them to the architect for his instructions. Clause 5.7 prohibits the contractor from using the documents except in connection with the works and neither employer, architect nor quantity surveyor must divulge the rates in the priced document.

viii)  **Statutory requirements**
As section 5.2.

ix)  **Site personnel**
As section 5.2.

x)  **Vesting of property**
As section 5.2.

xi)  **Insurance**
As section 5.2.

xii)  **Possession of site**
As section 5.2.

xiii)  **Completion, defects liability**
As section 5.2.

xiv)  **Extensions of time, damages for delay**
As section 5.2.

**5**  Selected contract terms

xv) **Partial completion**
As section 5.2.

xvi) **Assignment and sub-letting**
Similar to section 5.2 except that the list of three sub-contractors is inserted in either the specification or schedules of work, whichever is being used.

xvii) **Employer's licensees**
Similar to section 5.2 except that the work is or is not noted in the specification/schedules of work.

xviii) **Instructions**
As section 5.2.

xix) **Payment**
As section 5.2.

xx) **Variations and their valuation**
Variations are defined and rules set out for their valuation in clause 13. The basis of valuation is the rates in the priced document (that is either the priced specification, priced schedules of work, contract sum analysis or schedule of rates) including a fair allowance for any change in the conditions under which the work is carried out or change in quantity. Work not of similar character must be valued at fair rates and prices or on a daywork basis. The valuation must be carried out by the quantity surveyor.

xxi) **Loss and/or expense**
As section 5.2.

xxii) **Contract sum**
The work included in the contract sum can be ascertained by looking at the contract documents. If there are no quantities, the contract drawings and specification/schedules of work must be read together and, in the case of inconsistencies, the drawings prevail. If there are quantities in the specification/schedules of work, the quantities will prevail. Clause 3 stipulates that where adjustments are to be made to the contract sum, the amounts must be included in the next interim certificate after ascertainment takes place.

**5.4** JCT 80 Without Quantities

xxiii) Antiquities
As section 5.2.

xxiv) War
As section 5.2.

xxv) Termination
As section 5.2.

xxvi) Disputes
As section 5.2.

**5.5**
**IFC 84**

i) Type of contract
This is a traditional form of contract dealing with the situation where the architect prepares the production information and a quantity surveyor may be involved in the preparation of bills of quantities. The contractor tenders to carry out the work without any design responsibility. the architect should be working to a very tight brief where the entire scope and nature of the work is known although there is provision for variations in the work after commencement on site.

ii) The contract documents
- Contract drawings; and
- Printed form; and
- Particulars, where applicable, of the tender of any named person in NAM/T; and
either Priced specification/Priced schedules of work/Priced bills of quantities,
or Unpriced specification. (The contractor must supply either a contract sum analysis or a schedule of rates, neither of which are contract documents.)

iii) Type of price
As section 5.2.

iv) Provision for architect, etc.
As section 5.2.

v) Unusual provisions
Under clause 3.13 if any work, materials or goods are found not

**5** Selected contract terms

to be in accordance with the contract, the contractor must set out his proposals to the architect. These must show, at no cost to the employer, that there is no similar failure in any work carried out or materials and goods supplied. There is provision for the architect to issue instructions to open up if he is not satisfied with the contractor's proposals, if the contractor does not submit them within 7 days, or if for safety or statutory reasons the architect is unable to wait.

vi) Contractor's obligations
As section 5.2.

vii) Provision of information
The architect must provide the contractor with a copy of the contract documents, two copies of the contract drawings and the unpriced bills of quantities, specification or schedules of work, and with further drawings as may be necessary to enable the contractor to carry out and complete the works in accordance with the contract. Clause 1.3 provides that nothing in the specification/schedules of work/bills of quantities can override or modify the printed form. Errors or inconsistencies in or between the contract drawings and specification/schedules of work/bills of quantities are to be corrected and if the quality or quantity of the work is changed, the corrected version must be valued under clause 3.7. Where bills of quantities are included in the contract documents, they are to be prepared according to the Standard Method of Measurement of Building Works 7th edition. Clause 1.8 prohibits the contractor from using the documents except in connection with the works, and neither employer, architect nor quantity surveyor must divulge the rates in the contract bills.

viii) Statutory requirements
As section 5.2.

ix) Site personnel
Clause 3.4 stipulates that the contractor must keep a competent person-in-charge on the works at all reasonable times. The employer is entitled to employ a clerk of works who is under the directions of the architect and whose function is solely that of an inspector.

x) Vesting of property
Clause 1.10 sets out the rules. Unfixed materials delivered to

**5.5**   IFC 84

site may not be removed except with the architect's written consent. If the value is included in an interim certificate paid by the employer, he thereupon becomes the owner. Similar rules apply to materials stored off-site.

xi) Insurance

Clauses 6.1 and 6.2 provide for the contractor to indemnify the employer and take out insurance against personal injury or death except to the extent that it is due to the employer's negligence, and against damage to property (except the works) to the extent that it is due to the contractor's negligence. Provision is made in clause 6.2.4 for insurance to be taken out by the contractor, if the Appendix states it may be required and the architect so instructs, in respect of employer's losses because of damage to property other than the works where negligence is not involved. Clause 6.3 provides for insurance of the works. There are two categories of insurance:

- All risks; and
- Specified perils.

Specified perils includes the usual fire, lightning, explosion, storm, tempest and so on. All risks covers those and the additional risks of impact, subsidence, theft and vandalism.

Clause 6.3A applies to insurance of new works where the insurance is to be taken out by the contractor.

Clause 6.3B applies to insurance of new works where the insurance is to be taken out by the employer.

Clause 6.3C applies to works of alteration or extension to existing building where the insurance is to be taken out by the employer in regard to the existing and new part of the works.

All works insurance is to be in joint names against all risks except for insurance of existing buildings and contents, which are to be in joint names against specified perils. There are provisions in respect of the production of evidence of insurance and power to insure by the other party in case of default. The contractor is obliged to restore damaged work in every case, but there are important provisos:

- If the contractor insures new work, he receives in payment, via the employer by certificates, only the amounts paid by the insurers. Thus he has to stand the amount of any excess or under-insurance.
- If the employer insures new work, the contractor is entitled to receive proper payment as though the restoration is a variation. The employer has to stand the amount of any excess or under-insurance.

&bull; The situation is similar under clause 6.3C, but either party may determine the contractor's employment if it is just and equitable so to do.

Clause 6.3D provides, if it is stated in the Appendix that the employer may so require, for insurance to be taken out by the contractor. This insurance should provide payment to the employer of the amount of liquidated damages otherwise lost as a result of the architect granting the contractor an extension of time caused by a specified peril.

xii) Possession of the site

Possession of the site is dealt with by clause 2.1. The employer must give possession on the date stated in the contract. The contractor must begin the works and proceed regularly and diligently to completion. The employer may not take possession of any part of the works until practical completion, but if the contractor consents the employer may use the site for storage or other purposes subject to confirmation that the insurance cover will not be prejudiced. The employer may defer giving possession of the site, if the Appendix states that clause 2.2 applies, for the period stated in the Appendix (which should not exceed six weeks).

xiii) Completion, defects liability

Clause 2.1 makes clear that the contractor must complete the works on or before the contract completion date. When the architect is of the opinion that the works have achieved practical completion, clause 2.9 stipulates that he must issue a certificate to that effect. Among other things, the defects liability period then starts and the architect may notify the contractor of defects up to 14 days after the expiry of the period. After rectification of the defects, the architect issues a certificate of making good defects. However, this does not signal the release of the second half of the retention money.

xiv) Extensions of time, damages for delay

The contractor must notify the architect whenever the works are or are likely to be delayed, including the cause of the delay, and provide such information as the architect may reasonably require. The architect's duty is to grant a fair and reasonable extension of time as soon as he is able to estimate the length of delay beyond completion date caused by an event in clause 2.4. The architect has express power to grant an extension of time if one of the starred events noted below occurs after completion

**5.5**   IFC 84

date but before practical completion. He may also make an extension of time up to 12 weeks after practical completion, but he may not reduce previous extensions. The events may be summarised as follows:

- *Force majeure.*
- Exceptionally adverse weather.
- Damage due to specified perils.
- Civil commotion, strikes, etc.
- Compliance with architect's instructions.*
- Instructions to open up or test.*
- Late information.*
- Employer's men or materials.*
- Inability to obtain labour or materials (optional)
- Failure to give access.*
- Statutory undertakers.
- Deferment of possession.

If the contractor fails to complete the works by the contract completion date, the architect must issue a certificate to that effect, and the employer may then give notice in writing and deduct liquidated damages at the rate stated in the Appendix. There is express provision, in the event of a further extension being granted, for the architect to cancel his certificate of non-completion and issue a new one.

xv) Partial completion

There is a suggested additional clause in Practice Note IN/1 which is to be inserted as clause 2.11 if the employer wishes to take possession of part of the works before practical completion. The clause provides that if the employer, with the contractor's consent, does take such possession the consequences which follow are very much as though the part had achieved practical completion and the appropriate certificate had been issued. The architect, however, is not required to issue any written statement or certificate.

xvi) Assignment and sub-letting

Neither party may assign the contract.

Clause 3.2 allows the contractor to sub-let work with the architect's consent.

Clause 3.3 deals with named persons as sub-contractors. They can arise in two ways:

- If work is included in the contract documents to be priced by the contractor but to be carried out by the named person.
- If work is included in an architect's instruction regarding

**5**   Selected contract terms

the expenditure of a provisional sum and a person is named to carry it out.

There are then complicated provisions which vary depending upon the way in which the named sub-contractor has arisen. The terms provide for the situation if the sub-contractor refuses to enter in a sub-contract and if the contractor objects to the proposed named person under the second way of naming. If the named sub-contractor defaults and determination of his employment results, the contractor must notify the architect who must issue appropriate instructions. If the person was named in the contract documents and the instruction names another person, there may be an extension of time, but no loss and/or expense, and the contract sum is to be adjusted to cater for the difference in price. If the instruction omits the work or instructs the contractor to make his own arrangements, there may be an extension of time and loss and/or expense and the instruction ranks as a variation. If the person was named in an architect's instruction, a further instruction from the architect will give rise to an extension of time and loss and/or expense and payment as an instruction. If the reason for the sub-contractor's determination is a contractor's default, the provisions expressly exclude any increase in cost, extension of time or loss and/or expense. The contractor is obliged to take steps to recover from a defaulting sub-contractor additional costs and any liquidated damages deductible except for the extensions of time. These steps do not include legal proceedings unless the employer agrees to indemnify the contractor in respect of legal costs.

The contractor is not responsible to the employer for any design of the sub-contract works.

xvii) Employer's licensees
As section 5.2. The operative clause is 3.11.

xviii) Instructions
As 5.2 section except that there are no provisions for oral instructions.

xix) Payment
Governed by clause 4. Certificates must be issued at monthly intervals, unless a different period is inserted in the Appendix, until practical completion. Payment must be made by the employer within 14 days of a certificate issued by the architect. The value of work in a certificate must be at a date no earlier

**5.5**   IFC 84

than 7 days before certification. The retention is fixed at 5% until practical completion, when half the retention money is to be released. There is a tight schedule for issue of the final certificate. Within six months after practical completion the contractor must submit all documents for the final adjustment of the contract sum. A copy of the computations of the adjusted contract sum must be sent to the contractor not later than 3 months after receipt of the documents. The final certificate must be issued no more than 28 days from the later of:

- Issue of certificate of making good defects.
- Date final computations are sent to the contractor.

The employer has a further 28 days in which to pay. The final certificate is conclusive evidence, unless either party commences arbitration or other proceedings within 28 days of its issue, that:

- Quality and standards specified to be to architect's satisfaction are to his satisfaction.
- Contractual provisions requiring the adjustment of the contract sum have been carried out.
- Extensions of time have been properly given.
- Loss and/or expense is in final settlement of all contractor's claims on clause 4.12 matters.

Fluctuations are to be on the basis of supplemental condition C – contribution, levy and tax – unless supplemental condition D – price adjustment formula – is stated in the Appendix to apply.

xx) Variations and their valuation

Variations are defined in clause 3.6 and rules are set out for their valuation in clause 3.7. The basis for valuation is the rates in the priced document or pro-rata unless not appropriate, when a fair valuation must be made or a daywork basis may be used. Omitted work is generally valued at the rates in the priced document. The valuation must be carried out by the quantity surveyor.

xxi) Loss and/or expense

The contractor may claim direct loss and/or expense if the date for possession has been deferred or if regular progress has been or is likely to be substantially affected due to any of the following matters:

- Late information.
- Opening up and testing.
- Employer's men or materials.

**5** Selected contract terms

- Postponement.
- Failure to give access.
- Compliance with architect's instructions.
- Approximate quantity not a reasonably accurate forecast.

The contractor must make written application as soon as it is apparent that he has or is likely to incur direct loss and/or expense. He must supply, on request, reasonably necessary information.

xxii) Contract sum

The quality and quantity of work included in the contract documents is to be established according to the following rules:
- If there are any quantities, they prevail.
- If no quantities, the drawings prevail.
- Otherwise read all contract documents together.

Adjustments are authorised in 13 different places in the conditions.

xxiii) Antiquities

No provision.

xxiv) War

No express reference, but it would fall under references to *force majeure* in clauses 2.4.1 and 7.8.1(a).

xxv) Termination

Either party may determine the contractor's employment for stipulated reasons:

The employer, after written notice, if the contractor:
- wholly suspends work without reasonable cause; or
- fails to proceed regularly and diligently; or
- does not comply with notice to remove defective work and as a result the works are substantially affected; or
- fails to comply with clauses 3.2 or 3.3.

In the case of insolvency, determination is automatic.

The contractor, after written notice, if:
- the employer does not pay the amount due; or
- the employer interferes with a certificate; or
- the work is suspended for the period noted in the Appendix due to:
  - Architect's instructions; or
  - Late information; or
  - Employer's men or materials; or
  - Employer's failure to give access.

In the case of insolvency, the contractor may determine without notice.

Either party if the works are suspended for a period noted in the Appendix due to:

* *force majeure*; or
* loss or damage due to specified perils; or
* civil commotion.

The provisions are to be found in clauses 7.1, 7.5 and 7.8.

If the employer determines:

* The contractor must give up possession of the site.
* The employer may pay others to complete the work.
* The employer may use contractor's plant and/or require its removal from site.
* The employer may charge the contractor loss and/or expense and the difference in cost of having others to complete. He must value work done, but need not pay the contractor until the work is completed and accounts drawn up.

If the contractor determines:

* He must remove his plant from site.
* He must be paid costs of removal together with value of work carried out and any loss and/or expense.

If either party determines under clause 7.8, the situation is the same as if the contractor determines under clause 7.5 except that he cannot claim any loss or expense.

xxvi) Disputes
As section 5.2. The appropriate Article is 5.1 and clause 9.

## 5.6
## MW 80

i) Type of contract
This is a traditional form of contract dealing with the situation where the architect prepares the production information and the contractor tenders to carry out the work with design responsibility. The entire scope and nature of the work should be known at time of tender, although there is provision for variations in the work after commencement on site.

ii) The contract documents
* printed form; and
* contract drawings; and/or

**5** Selected contract terms

- specification; and/or
- schedules.

iii) Type of price
As section 5.2.

iv) Provision for architect, etc.
The first recital provides for the insertion of the name of the architect or the contract administrator depending on whether the person is registered under the Architects Registration Acts 1931 to 1969. The fourth recital makes reference to a quantity surveyor, but he is given no express powers or duties within the conditions.

v) Unusual provisions
The fifth recital and supplementary memorandum part E provides for a guarantee/warranty scheme to apply (the BEC Guarantee Scheme) if the employer so wishes. Part E makes amendment to certain insurance clauses and incorporates the 'scheme documents' as part of the contract.

vi) Contractor's obligations
These are principally contained in clause 1.1 to carry out and complete the works in accordance with the contract documents. There is a proviso to the effect that if approval of the quality of materials or the standard of workmanship is to be left to the architect, he must exercise his function reasonably. The final certificate is not conclusive on this point.

vii) Provision of information
The architect must issue the contractor with any further information necessary for the proper carrying out of the works. Clause 4.1 provides that nothing contained in the drawings, specification or schedules overrides, modifies or affects the printed form. Inconsistencies in or between the contract documents are to be corrected and if it results in an addition, reduction or change, it is to be treated as a variation. In view of the wording of clause 1.1, there are likely to be few variations on this account.

viii) Statutory requirements
As section 5.2 except that there is no provision for emergency compliance.

**5.6**  MW 80

ix) Site personnel

Clause 3.3 stipulates that the contractor must keep a competent person in charge on the works at all reasonable times. The architect is empowered by clause 3.4 to issue instructions requiring the contractor to exclude any employee from the works. There is no provision for a clerk of works.

x) Vesting of property

No provision.

xi) Insurance

Clause 6.1 provides for the contractor to indemnify the employer and take out insurance against personal injury or death except to the extent that it is due to the employer's negligence; clause 6.2 provides for the contractor to indemnify the employer and take out insurance against damage to property (except the works) to the extent that it is due to the employer's negligence.

Clause 6.3 provides for the insurance of the works. There is only one category of insurance: against fire, lightning, explosion, storm, tempest, etc. similar to 'specified perils' under JCT 80.

Clause 6.3A applies to insurance of new works. The insurance is to be taken out by the contractor in joint names.

Clause 6.3B applies to existing structures. The insurance is to be taken out by the employer in joint names.

The party with responsibility to insure may be required by the other to produce evidence that the insurance is in force.

If the contractor insures, he receives in payment, via the employer by certificates, only the amounts paid by the insurers. Thus he has to stand the amount of any excess or under-insurance. If the employer insures, the contractor is entitled to receive proper payment as though the restoration is a variation.

xii) Possession of the site

Possession of the site is dealt with by implication in clause 2.1. The employer must give possession to enable the contractor to commence on the stated date. The contractor may commence on that date, but he must proceed with due diligence to completion.

xiii) Completion, defects liability

Clause 2.1 stipulates that the contractor must complete by the completion date. The architect must certify practical completion when in his opinion the works have reached that

**5**   Selected contract terms

stage. Half the retention must be released within 14 days and, among other things, the defects liability period starts and the contractor has an obligation to rectify defects, excessive shrinkages or other faults which appear during the period. At the end of the period, the architect must certify when the contractor has discharged his obligations.

xiv) Extensions of time, damages for delay
The contractor must notify the architect if it becomes apparent that the works will not be complete by the due date for reasons beyond the contractor's control including compliance with any architect's instruction provided that it is not issued as a result of the contractor's default. The architect's duty is then to make a reasonable extension of time. If the contractor fails to complete by the completion date, the employer may deduct liquidated damages at the rate stated in the Appendix.

xv) Partial completion
No provision.

xvi) Assignment and sub-letting
Neither party may assign the contract and the contractor may not sub-let without the architect's written consent.

xvii) Employer's licensees
No provision.

xviii) Instructions
Under the provisions of clause 3.5 the architect may issue written instructions. The contractor must carry out the work forthwith. The architect may issue a 7 day compliance notice and the employer may engage others to do the work. Oral instructions must be confirmed in two days by the architect.

xix) Payment
If so requested by the contractor, the architect must certify progress payments in respect of work properly carried out at not less than four weekly intervals. The employer has 14 days in which to pay. Retention is fixed at 5% until practical completion when it reduces to 2.5% until the final certificate. Within 3 months of practical completion, the contractor must supply all documentation for computation of the final sum. Provided the architect has issued the certificate under clause 2.5, the final certificate must be issued within 28 days of receipt of

the contractor's documentation.

Optional clause 4.5 provides for fluctuations in respect of contribution levy and tax changes. In other respects the contract is on a fixed-price basis.

xx) Variations and their valuation
The rules for variations are set out in clause 3.6. They are to be valued on a fair and reasonable basis using relevant rates in the priced document. Alternatively, the price may be agreed between architect and contractor before the work is carried out.

xxi) Loss and/or expense
There is no machinery entitling the contractor to make application under the contract, but clause 3.6 expressly provides that the valuation of any variation may include any direct loss and/or expense due to regular progress being affected by compliance with an instruction.

xxii) Contract sum
The quality and quantity of the work is to be determined by looking at the contract documents as a whole. This is clear from Article 1 and clauses 1.1 and 4.1. Adjustment to the contract sum is authorised in eight different places in the conditions.

xxiii) Antiquities
No provision.

xxiv) War
No provision.

xxv) Termination
Either party may determine the contractor's employment for stipulated reasons:
The employer if the contractor:
- wholly suspends work without reasonable cause; or
- fails to proceed diligently; or
- becomes insolvent.
The contractor, after written notice, if the employer:
- fails to pay the amount due; or
- interferes with a certificate; or
- suspends the carrying out of the work for a month.
Without notice if the employer becomes insolvent.
The provisions are to be found in clauses 7.1 and 7.2.

5   Selected contract terms

The consequences of determination involve:

If the employer determines:

- He is not bound to make any further payment to the contractor until after the completion of the works.
- The contractor must immediately give up possession of the site.

If the contractor determines:

- the employer must pay a fair and reasonable sum for work done, materials on site and removal of equipment.

xxvi) Disputes

The procedure for dealing with disputes is to be arbitration. Article 4 and clause 9 apply. Either party may require a dispute to be referred by giving written notice to the other. If there is no agreement on the arbitrator, the President or Vice-President of either the RIBA or the RICS can be asked to nominate. The arbitrator has wide powers to order rectification of the contract and open up any certificate or decision of the architect. By optional clause 9.5 arbitrations are to be conducted under the JCT Arbitration Rules 1987.

## 5.7
## JCT 81 With Contractor's Design

i) Type of contract

This is essentially a package deal contract where the contractor is responsible for design and construction of the project, preparation of production information, and construction.

ii) The contract documents

- employer's requirements; and
- contractor's proposals; and
- contract sum analysis; and
- printed form.

iii) Type of price

As section 5.2.

iv) Provision for architect, etc.

There is no architect or quantity surveyor, but there is provision, in article 3, for the employer to appoint an agent to give and receive notices, applications, instructions and so on, and otherwise act for the employer under any of the conditions.

v) Unusual provisions

Clause 2.3.1 provides that any divergence between the Employer's Requirements and the definition of the site boundary by the employer under clause 7 will be corrected by the employer's instruction, which will be treated as a change.

vi) Contractor's obligations

These are principally contained in clause 2.1 to carry out and complete the works referred to in the contract documents, and for that purpose to complete the design for the works including the selection of specification (so far as not described in the Employer's Requirements or Contractor's Proposals). Clause 2.5 spells out the contractor's design obligation in more detail. His liability is similar to that of an architect. He is not guaranteeing fitness for purpose. Moreover, if the work does not involve dwellings, his liability is further restricted to the amount stated in Appendix 1.

vii) Provision of information

The employer must provide the contractor with copies of the contract documents, but it is for the contractor under clause 5.3 to provide the employer with two copies of the information which he prepares in order to carry out the works. Where the optional supplementary provisions are in use, the employer can set out in his Requirements whatever procedure he may wish to impose in respect of drawing submission. It is made clear that the employer may comment, but that his comments will not affect the contractor's liability for the work unless the comments specifically so state. Clause 2.2.1 provides that nothing in the Employer's Requirements, the Contractor's Proposals or the Contract Sum Analysis will override or modify the printed form. If there is a discrepancy within the Employer's Requirements, the Contractor's Proposals will prevail, but if they do not deal with the problem, the contractor must put forward his proposal. The employer can notify the contractor of his agreement or his own solution, either of which will be treated as a change. If there is a discrepancy within the Contractor's Proposals, the contractor must put forward his proposals. The employer can choose between the discrepant items or the contractor's suggestion at no extra cost. Clause 5.6 prohibits either party from divulging any of the documents or using them for any purpose other than the works.

**5**  Selected contract terms

viii) Statutory requirements
Generally as section 5.2 except that the employer is substituted for the architect, also: if either party finds a divergence between the documents and statutory requirements it must be notified to the other. The contractor must complete the design and construction of the works in accordance with his proposed amendment if the employer consents. Changes in statutory requirements after the base date will be treated as changes, as will any amendments necessary to conform with the terms of any development control authority permission.

ix) Site personnel
The contractor must keep a competent person-in-charge constantly on the works. There is no provision for a clerk of works. Where the Supplementary Provisions apply, the employer's consent is required before the appointment of a site manager and he must not be replaced without the employer's further consent. The site manager and any other of the contractor's servants, agents or sub-contractors must attend site meetings as reasonably requested by the employer.

x) Vesting of property
As section 5.2.

xi) Insurance
As section 5.2. There is no provision for the contractor to take out and maintain professional indemnity insurance in respect of his design responsibilities.

xii) Possession of the site
As section 5.2.

xiii) Completion, defects liability
As section 5.2 except that the employer issues a written statement when practical completion has been reached, and notifies the contractor (rather than certifies), when making good of defects has been completed.

xiv) Extensions of time, damages for delay
As section 5.2 except that the employer is substituted for the architect. Delay by nominated sub-contractors and approximate quantities, not being an accurate forecast, are deleted from the list of relevant events; delay in receiving statutory approvals and delay due to change in statutory requirements after the base date is added.

**5.7**   JCT 81 With Contractor's Design

xv) Partial completion
As section 5.2 except that the employer is substituted for the architect.

xvi) Assignment and sub-letting
Neither party may assign the contract, but the employer may assign to any future purchaser or lessee the right to bring proceedings if Appendix 1 so states.

Clause 18.2 allows the contractor to sub-let work or design with the employer's consent. There is no provision for nominated, named or listed sub-contractors.

If the Supplementary Provisions are used, the employer may name persons in the Employer's Requirements who are to be employed as a sub-contractor. The provisions are very similar to the naming provisions in IFC 84 (see section 5.5). If the named sub-contractor's employment is determined, the contractor must complete the work himself and it is treated as a change unless the determination is due to the contractor's default.

xvii) Employer's licensees
As section 5.2.

xviii) Instructions
As section 5.2.

xix) Payment
Complex provisions governed by clause 30. Interim payments must be made by the employer in accordance with either alternative A stage payments or alternative B periodic payments. In each case, the contractor must first make application. Periodic payments are usually at monthly intervals until practical completion, and stage payments are at whatever stages the parties decide and note in the Appendix. The employer must make payment within 14 days of the date of issue of the application for payment unless:
- the application is not accompanied by the details stated in the Employer's Requirements; and/or
- the employer disputes the amount in which case he must pay the amount he considers properly due.

Retention money must be deposited in a special bank account if the contractor so requests. Retention must be released, half at practical completion, the other half at certification of making good defects.

5   Selected contract terms

There is a tight schedule for the finalisation of accounts. The contractor must submit the final account and final statement within three months of practical completion, together with supporting documents. If the employer agrees, or if it is not disputed, it becomes conclusive as to the balance due between the parties on the last of the following:

- one month from the end of the defects liability period; or
- one month from completion of making good defects; or
- one month from the submission of the final account and final statement with all supporting details.

If the contractor fails to submit the final account and final statement by the due date, the employer may give written notice and two months later himself prepare the final account and final statement. If the contractor does not dispute it, the final account and final statement is conclusive as to the balance between the parties on the latest of the following:

- one month from the end of the defects liability period; or
- one month from completion of making good defects; or
- one month from the sending of the final account and final statement to the contractor by the employer.

Apart from the balance owing between the parties, the final account and final statement is also conclusive evidence, unless either party commences arbitration or other proceedings within 28 days of issue, that:

- Quality and standards stated in the Employer's Requirements to be to the employer's satisfaction are to his satisfaction.
- Extensions of time have been properly given.
- Loss and/or expense is in final settlement of all contractor's claims on clause 26 matters.

Fluctuations are the subject of optional clauses 36, 37 or 38 which allow fluctuations for contribution, levy and tax; labour and materials cost; or the use of price adjustment formula respectively.

xx) Variations and their valuation

As section 5.2 with the following exceptions: Variations are referred to as 'changes' as defined in clause 12. There is no reference to the person responsible for carrying out the valuation. If the Supplementary Provisions are used, the procedure is simplified. If the contractor considers that an instruction will entail valuation, extension of time or loss and/or expense, he must submit estimates within 14 days unless the employer states that they are not required or the contractor objects. The parties must try to agree the estimates. If they fail

**5.7**  JCT 81 With Contractor's Design

to agree, the employer may withdraw the instruction, refer the matter to the adjudicator or instruct compliance, and this provision will not apply.

xxi) **Loss and/or expense**

The contractor may claim direct loss and/or expense if the date for possession has been deferred or if regular progress has been or is likely to be substantially affected due to any of the following matters:

- Late information.
- Opening up and testing.
- Employer's men or materials.
- Postponement.
- Failure to give access.
- Compliance with employer's instructions.
- Delay in development control permission.

The contractor must make written application as soon as it is apparent that regular progress is or is likely to be affected. He must supply, on request, information as the employer reasonably requires.

If the Supplementary Provisions are in use, the provisions of clause 26 are modified. The contractor must submit an estimate to the employer with the next application for payment. He must continue to submit estimates with each application for payment so long as the loss and/or expense continues to be incurred. The employer has 21 days in which to notify the contractor that he accepts, that he wishes to negotiate, or that the provisions of clause 26 are to apply. An acceptance, agreement or adjudicator's decision is truly final in respect of the matter during the period under consideration. Failure to submit estimates results in the loss and/or expense being ascertained under clause 26, but no adjustment to the contract sum may take place until the final account.

xxii) **Contract sum**

The quality and quantity of the work is deemed to be that set out in the Employer's Requirements and the Contractor's Proposals. Clause 3 stipulates that where adjustments are to be made to the contract sum, the amounts must be included in the next interim certificate after ascertainment takes place. Adjustment is authorised in 19 different places in the conditions.

xxiii) **Antiquities**

As section 5.2 except the contractor must notify the employer

**5** Selected contract terms

who must issue the appropriate instructions.

xxiv) War
As section 5.2.

xxv) Termination
As section 5.2 with the following differences:
There is no ground for determination by the contractor for employer's interference with a certificate, or for employer's insolvency.

Another cause of suspension is delay in receipt of Development Control permission.

If the employer determines, the contractor must provide him with two copies of all drawings completed before determination, and the employer may pay others to carry out and complete the design and construction of the works.

xxvi) Disputes
As section 5.2 except that there is no procedure for joining arbitrations on related matters.

Where the Supplementary Provisions are used, a dispute which falls into the category of an 'adjudication matter' has first to be referred to an adjudicator who makes a speedy decision. Only if a party objects to the decision can arbitration take place, but not until after practical completion of the works.

## 5.8 JCT Fixed Fee Form of Prime Cost Contract

i) Type of contract
This is a form of contract dealing with the situation where the architect prepares the production information and the contractor tenders on the basis of a fixed fee to carry out the work without any design responsibility. The nature and scope of the works must be known, but not the details nor the extent.

ii) The contract documents
- specification;
- printed form; and
- drawings

are delayed, including the cause of delay. The architect's duty is to make a fair and reasonable extension of time as soon as he is able to estimate the delay beyond the date for completion, if in his opinion the reason for the delay is:

- *Force majeure.*
- Exceptionally inclement weather.
- Damage due to insured risks.
- Civil commotion, strikes, etc.
- Compliance with architect's instructions.
- Late information.
- Delay by nominated sub-contractors.
- Employer's men.
- Opening up and testing.
- Inability to obtain labour or materials.
- Antiquities.
- Statutory undertakers.

If the contractor fails to complete the works by the contract or extended completion date, and the architect issues a certificate to that effect, the employer may serve notice and deduct liquidated damages at the rate stated in the Appendix.

xv) Partial completion

Clause 12 allows the employer to take possession of part of the works with the contractor's consent. The architect must issue a certificate stating his estimate of the approximate prime cost of the part. Various consequences follow in respect of the part, very much as though the part had achieved practical completion and the relevant certificate had been issued.

xvi) Assignment and sub-letting

Neither party may assign the contract. Clause 13(3) allows the contractor to sub-let with the architect's consent which must expressly approve the method of charge. The architect may impose any conditions he sees fit.

Clause 23 provides for nomination of sub-contractors. There are procedures for payment and extensions of time, but there is no provision for renomination.

xvii) Employer's licensees

Clause 25 provides that the employer may engage other contractors to work on the site. The employer does not appear to be limited to work in the sixth schedule. The contractor's consent is not required.

**5**   Selected contract terms

xviii) Instructions

Clause 3 deals with instructions. The architect may issue such instructions as he thinks fit. He may not issue an instruction requiring an alteration in the nature or scope of the works. The contractor must carry out the work forthwith. The architect may issue a 7 day compliance notice and the employer may engage others. There is no provision for the contractor to challenge the validity of an instruction except through the medium of arbitration. Oral instructions must be confirmed by the contractor or the architect.

xix) Payment

Certificates must be issued in accordance with the time period in the Appendix (normally one month) until practical completion. Payment must be made by the employer within 14 days of a certificate issued by the architect. The value of work in a certificate must be as at a date no earlier than 7 days before certification. Retention must be released, half at practical completion and half at certification of making good defects. Provided that the contractor submits all required documents within a reasonable period after practical completion, the architect or the quantity surveyor must ascertain the prime cost before the end of the period of final ascertainment of prime cost in the Appendix. The architect must issue his final certificate no later than three months after the latest of:

- The end of the defects liability period.
- The completion of making good defects.
- Receipt by the architect of all documents necessary for ascertainment of the prime cost of the works.

The final certificate is conclusive evidence, unless either party commences arbitration or other proceedings within 14 days of the date of issue, that:

- Quality and standards specified to be to the architect's satisfaction are to his satisfaction.
- Contractual provisions regarding payment have been complied with.

There are, of course, no provisions for fluctuations.

xx) Variations and their valuation

Not applicable.

xxi) Loss and/or expense

The contractor may claim direct loss and/or expense if regular

**5.8** JCT Fixed Fee Form of Prime Cost Contract

progress has been substantially affected due to any of the following:
- Late information.
- Opening up and testing.
- Employer's men.
- Architect's instructions in regard to order of work or postponement.

The contractor must make written application within a reasonable time of it becoming apparent that the progress of the work has been affected.

xxii) Contract sum

There is no contract sum, but there is an estimate inserted into the third schedule. The quality of the work is set out in the specification.

xxiii) Antiquities

As section 5.2.

xxiv) War

As section 5.2.

xxv) Termination

Either party may determine the contractor's employment for stipulated reasons:

The employer, after written notice, if the contractor:
- wholly suspends work without reasonable cause; or
- fails to proceed regularly and diligently; or
- does not comply with notice to remove defective work and as a result the works are substantially affected; or
- fails to comply with clause 13.

In the case of insolvency, determination is automatic.

The contractor if:
- the employer does not pay amount due after notice; or
- the employer interferes with a certificate; or
- the work is suspended for the period noted in the Appendix due to:
  - *force majeure*; or
  - damage due to insured risks; or
  - civil commotion; or
  - architect's instructions; or
  - late information; or
  - employer's men; or
  - opening up of work.

**5** Selected contract terms

- the employer is insolvent.

The provisions are to be found in clauses 21 and 22.

The consequences of determination involve:

If the employer determines:

- He may pay others to complete the work.
- He may require the contractor to assign his rights in contracts with sub-contractors or suppliers.
- He may use contractor's plant and/or require its removal.
- He may charge the contractor loss and/or damage and the difference in cost of having others to complete. He need not make any further payment to the contractor until the work is completed and accounts drawn up.

If the contractor determines:

- He must remove his plant from site.
- He must be paid the costs of removal together with prime cost of work carried out, an appropriate proportion of the fee, and any loss and/or expense.

xxvi) Disputes

The procedure for dealing with disputes is to be arbitration. Clause 31 applies. All disputes are to be referred to arbitration. If there is no agreement on the arbitrator, the President or Vice-President of the RIBA can be asked to nominate. There is no provision for joining related arbitrations. The arbitrator has wide powers to open up any certificate or decision of the architect. Except by agreement, arbitration cannot be opened until after practical completion, termination or abandonment of the work except in specified instances.

## 5.9
## JCT 87 Management Contract

i) Type of contract

This is a form of contract dealing with the situation where the professional team prepares the production information and the contractor is appointed at an early stage to collaborate in the pre-construction process. His tender is on the basis of a fixed fee based on a contract cost plan. The contractor carries out a purely management function, all the work is carried out by the works contractors. The management contractor has no design responsibility.

ii) The contract documents

- project drawings; and

- project specification; and
- contract cost plan; and
- printed form and schedules.

iii) Type of price
Prime cost and the management contractor's fee. In principle, the contractor is paid the work contracts sums, the prime cost of his on-site staff and so on, and the prime cost of all materials and so on, provided for the work by the contractor, together with his fee for his management role.

iv) Provision for architect, etc.
As section 5.2 and provision is also made for the insertion of the names of other members of the professional team in article 5. The architect may add other persons to this list at any time provided that he notifies the contractor in writing.

v) Unusual provisions
Clause 3.21 provides that in the case of a breach of the works contract by a works contractor the contractor must:
- Operate the terms of the works contract for dealing with such breach, including arbitration or litigation to recover amounts due to the employer.
- Engage a further works contractor to complete works if such action is in accordance with the terms of the works contract or is necessary because of determination.
- Meet the proper claims of other works contractors as a result of the breach.

The employer must:
- Pay the contractor all amounts properly incurred in operating the terms of the works contract or engaging another works contractor.
- Keep an account of liquidated damages due as a result of the works contractor's breach, but not recover them from the contractor except to the extent that the contractor is able to recover them from the works contractor.

The employer may recover amounts due from the contractor only to the extent that the contractor has been able to recover them from the works contractor.

The contractor may deduct amounts paid to other contractors from monies due to the works contractor in breach, and must try to recover by arbitration or litigation if necessary, but any shortfall must be reimbursed by the employer. This clause offers complete protection to the contractor.

**5**   Selected contract terms

vi) Contractor's obligations
Principally set out in clauses 1.4 to 1.8 inclusive to:

- Co-operate with the professional team during the pre-construction stage.
- Manage the carrying out and completion of the project.
- Prepare programmes.
- Enter into works contracts in good time.
- Ensure the works contracts work is in accordance with project specification and works contracts. If the approval of the quality of materials or the standard of workmanship is to be left to the architect, he must exercise his satisfaction reasonably. The final certificate is conclusive evidence that, where the architect has left such matters for his satisfaction, he is so satisfied.
- Provide facilities as shown in the fifth schedule.
- Provide continual supervision.
- Ensure economical work.
- Keep goods records.
- Be liable to employer for any breach including works contractors' breaches.
- Forthwith secure compliance with instructions.

vii) Provision of information
The architect must provide the contractor with a copy of the contract documents. He must also provide all necessary further information to enable the project to be carried out and completed in accordance with the contract. There is no clause stipulating priority of documents. Clause 1.11 prohibits the contractor from using the documents except in connection with the project, and neither the employer nor any of the professional team must divulge any rates or the management fee.

viii) Statutory requirements
As section 5.2.

ix) Site personnel
Clause 3.1 stipulates that the contractor must employ on the project the management personnel listed in the attachment to the second schedule, these may not be changed without the architect's consent. Clause 3.13 further stipulates that the contractor must keep constantly on site a competent manager who must be approved by the architect and who must not be changed without the architect's approval. The architect is empowered to issue instructions ordering the removal of the

**5.9** JCT 87 Management Contract

manager. The employer is entitled to employ a clerk of works who is under the directions of the architect and whose duty is to act solely as an inspector.

x) Vesting of property
As section 5.2.

xi) Insurance
As section 5.2 except that there is no option for the employer to take out insurance for new work; whether or not the contractor insures, he is entitled to receive payment for restoration as though the restoration was a variation. There is no provision for the employer to take out insurance if the contractor defaults.

xii) Possession of the site
Possession of the site is dealt with by clause 2.3. Before that, the contractor must have initialled alterations to the third schedule, and signed part 2 of the Appendix. Following this, the architect notifies the employer of the date it will be practicable to start construction. The employer has 14 days in which to notify the contractor if he is to proceed. Failure to notify or notification that the employer does not wish to proceed is deemed determination of the contractor's employment. If the contractor is to proceed, he must have possession of the site on the date stated in the Appendix. The contractor must secure the commencement of the project and its diligent progress to completion. The employer may not take possession of any part of the project until practical completion, but if the contractor consents, the employer may use the site for storage or other purposes subject to confirmation that the insurance cover will not be prejudiced. The employer may defer giving possession of the site, if the Appendix states that clause 2.3.2 applies, for no more than six weeks.

xiii) Completion, defects liability
As section 5.2.

xiv) Extensions of time, damages for delay
The contractor must notify the architect whenever the completion date is not likely to be or has not been achieved, including the cause of the delay. The architect must give a fair and reasonable extension of time as soon as he can assess the delay beyond the due date caused by any of the project extension items. After the first exercise of his duty, he may reduce

5   Selected contract terms

extensions by taking omissions of work into account. The project extension items may be summarised as follows:

- Any cause which prevents the contractor properly carrying out his duties under the contract including:
  – Employer's default.
  – Late information.
  – Deferment of possession.
- Any relevant event (except delay by other works contractors) which entitles a works contractor to an extension of time.

The contractor must notify the architect of any decision to grant a works contractor an extension of time. The architect's consent is not required, but his dissent, if any, must be conveyed to the works contractor.

If the contractor fails to complete the works by the contract or extended completion date, the architect must issue a certificate to that effect, and the employer may then give notice and deduct liquidated damages at the rate stated in the Appendix. The power of recovery or deduction is subject to the provisions of clause 3.21 (see (v)).

xv) Partial completion
As section 5.2.

xvi) Assignment and sub-letting
Neither party may assign the contract, but the employer may assign to any future purchaser or lessee the right to bring proceedings if the Appendix so states.

Clause 8.2.1 stipulates that works contractors are to be chosen by agreement between the architect and the contractor, and the architect then issues an instruction. The whole of the physical work is divided into works contract packages. The architect must direct the amounts payable to the works contractors, and there are provisions to cover practical completion of the works contracts and the contractor's duties under each works contract.

xvii) Employer's licensees
As section 5.2.

xvii) Instructions
Under the provisions of clause 3.3 the architect may issue such instructions as are reasonably necessary to enable the contractor properly to discharge his duties. Unless it concerns a change in

**5.9**   JCT 87 Management Contract

design, quality or quantity of work in the works contract, or the imposition of obligations or restrictions in regard to access or sequence of work and so on, the contractor must secure the carrying out of the instruction forthwith. If the contractor on behalf of a works contractor questions an empowering clause, it is deemed valid if he thereafter complies. Oral instructions may be confirmed by either the architect or the contractor.

xix)   Payment
Certificates must be issued in accordance with the time periods in the Appendix. Payment must be made by the employer within 14 days of a certificate issued by the architect. The scheme of payments is divided into pre-construction and construction periods. During the pre-construction period, the amounts certified will be an appropriate instalment of the management fee. During the construction period, the amounts will be amounts payable under works contracts, an appropriate instalment of the management fee, and any other proper costs incurred by the contractor. Unless the employer is a local authority, the contractor or any works contractor may require retention to be placed in a separate bank account. Retention must be released: half at practical completion, and half at certification of making good defects. The construction period management fee may be adjusted by reference to a formula if the prime cost differs from the contract cost plan total by more than 5%. Within six months of practical completion, the contractor must submit all documents necessary to ascertain the prime cost. Within three months of receipt of the documents, the quantity surveyor must give the architect a statement of the prime cost and management fee, which the architect must pass to the contractor. The final certificate must be issued not more than two months after the latest of:
- Completion of making good defects.
- End of the defects liability period.
- The receipt by the architect of the statement of prime cost and management fee.

The final certificate is conclusive evidence, unless either party commences arbitration or other proceedings within 28 days of its issue, that:
- Quality and standards specified to the architect's satisfaction are to his satisfaction.
- Contractual provisions with regard to payment have been carried out.
- Extensions of time have been properly given.

**5**   Selected contract terms

- Loss and/or expense is in final settlement of all works contractors' claims.

Fluctuations are dealt with under the separate works contracts.

xx)  Variations and their valuation
Not applicable.

xxi)  Loss and/or expense
There is no provision for contractor's claims, but there is provision in clause 8.5 for the contractor to pass on claims from works contractors. It is for the architect to form an opinion and ascertain or instruct the quantity surveyor to ascertain the amount of such loss and/or expense in collaboration with the contractor.

xxii)  Contract sum
There is no contract sum, but there is a contract cost plan total. The quality and quantity of the work is determined by the works contract packages.

xxiii)  Antiquities
As section 5.2.

xxiv)  War
No express provision.

xxv)  Termination
As section 5.2 and the employer may determine the contractor's employment at will by simply giving notice in writing. The consequences are that the employer must indemnify the contractor against any valid claims by works contractors; the contractor may be required to assign his rights in contracts for work or goods; and the contractor is entitled to payment of an appropriate portion of the pre-construction period management fee if determination takes place during the pre-construction period. If it takes place during the construction period, the consequences will be the same as if the contractor had determined. The provisions are to be found in section 7 (clauses 7.1 to 7.13 inclusive).

xxvi)  Disputes
As section 5.2.

**5.9**  JCT 87 Management Contract

**5.10**
**ACA 2**

i) Type of contract
This is essentially a traditional form of contract which, by the deletion of optional clauses, can present itself in varied aspects. Either architect or contractor can be responsible for the preparation of detailed production information. The contractor may therefore take no, some or virtually the whole of the design responsibility. Essentially, the architect should be working to a very tight brief where the entire scope and nature of the work is known, although there is provision for variations in the work after commencement on site.

ii) The contract documents
- contract drawings; and
- time schedule; and
- printed form; and
- schedule of rates; or
- contract bills; and/or
- specification.

iii) Type of price
Lump sum. In principle, this is a fixed price contract, although the contract provisions soften this effect as far as the contractor is concerned, for example by providing for fluctuations to varying degrees, and the adjustment of the contract sum as a result of variations.

iv) Provision for architect and so on
Recital E provides for the insertion of the name of the architect or, in alternative two, the name of the supervising officer if he is an unregistered person. Optional clause 15.2 provides for the insertion of the name of the quantity surveyor. The employer may nominate another person to act in each case, but the contractor has the right of objection.

v) Unusual provisions
Clause 11.8 gives the architect power to order the contractor to accelerate the works.

vi) Contractor's obligations
Principally contained in clause 1.1 to carry out and complete the works in strict accordance with the contract documents. Clause

**5**    Selected contract terms

1.2 requires the contractor to use the skill and care of a contractor qualified and experienced in carrying out work of a similar size and scope to the works. If the contractor is to be responsible for any element of design, his responsibilities are spelled out in clause 3.1, to design in conformity with any performance specification, and so as to be fit for purpose.

vii) Provision of information

Either the architect or the contractor may be responsible for the provision of production information. Clause 2 in one of its options applies. The information is to be provided in accordance with the dates set out in the time schedule. This is similar to the appendix of JCT forms, but it contains a schedule for the provision of information, listing the dates by which the information is required and the party responsible for provision. Clause 1.3 provides that the printed form prevails over any other contract document except as expressly noted. Neither the employer nor the contractor must divulge or make use of documents except for the works, neither must they divulge any prices in the schedule of rates or the contract bills.

viii) Statutory requirements

Clause 1.7 states that the contractor must comply with and give all notices and pay all fees required by statute and so on. Except where the contractor supplies production information, in which case he is responsible for ensuring compliance with statutory requirements, he must report all divergences to the architect, who must issue instructions. There is no express provision for emergency compliance with statutory requirements.

ix) Site personnel

Clause 5 refers to site supervision and provides that the contractor, with the architect's consent, must appoint a manager on site; this manager cannot be changed without the architect's further consent. The contractor must employ properly qualified and experienced trade operatives and the architect may request the presence of any of the site personnel at meetings in connection with the works. Clause 8.1(b) empowers the architect to order the dismissal from the works of any incompetent person.

x) Vesting of property

The rules are set out in clause 6.1. Once incorporated into the works, materials become the property of the employer. If

**5.10**   ACA 2

provision is to be made for payment for goods before incorporation, the optional part of the clause provides that the employer owns the goods after paying a certificate including the value. By clause 6.2, the risk of loss or damage remains with the contractor until after taking over the works.

xi) Insurance

Clause 6.3 provides for the contractor to indemnify the employer and take out insurance against personal injury or death, except to the extent that it is due to the employer's negligence, and against damage to property (except the works) to the extent that it is due to the contractor's negligence. Provision is made in clause 6.5 for insurance to be taken out by the contractor, if the contract documents so require, in respect of employer's losses because of damage to property other than the works where negligence is not involved.

Clause 6.4 provides in one of two options for the contractor to take out insurance for new work. Alternative two provides for the employer to take out insurance in the case of work to existing buildings. All insurance is to be in joint names against the contingencies specified in the respective policies. There is provision for the contractor to produce documentary evidence of the insurance, and for the employer to insure himself if the contractor defaults. The contractor is obliged to restore damaged work whoever insures, but there are important provisos:

- If the contractor insures new work, he receives in payment, via the employer by certificates, only the amounts paid by the insurers. Thus he has to stand the amount of any underinsurance or excess.
- If the employer insures, the contractor is entitled to receive proper payment, and the employer must stand the amount of any under-insurance or excess.

An optional clause 6.6 requires the contractor to take out design indemnity insurance with a limit of indemnity to be stated in the contract documents.

xii) Possession of the site

Possession of the site is dealt with by clause 11.1. The employer must give possession on the date stated in the time schedule. The contractor must begin work and proceed regularly and in accordance with the time schedule to completion. The employer may not take possession of any part of the works until taking over occurs, except that provision can be made in the time schedule for sectional completion of the works.

**5**   Selected contract terms

xiii) Completion, defects liability

Clause 11.1 makes clear that the contractor must complete the works on the date for taking over. When the contractor considers the works are fit and ready for taking over, he must notify the architect accompanied, if appropriate, by a list of outstanding work. The architect may either:

- issue a taking over certificate; or
- give the contractor a list of work required to render the works fit and ready for taking over; or
- approve the contractor's list; and/or
- add to the contractor's list at any time before taking over.

The architect may issue a taking over certificate if the contractor issues a written undertaking to the employer to complete items in either or both lists on issue of the certificate. Among other things, the maintenance period then starts and the architect may send details of defects to the contractor throughout the period and up to ten days thereafter.

xiv) Extensions of time, damages for delay

The contractor is required to notify the architect whenever taking over the works on the due date is likely to be prevented, including the circumstances of the delay and an estimate of the extension to which he considers himself entitled. The architect's duty, after the contractor has proved to his satisfaction that taking over of the works is prevented, is to grant the extension as soon as practicable. In any case this may be no later than 60 days after receipt of all particulars unless relating to employer's default, when the extension may be given at any time.

The architect must review the extensions within a reasonable time after taking over the works. He may fix a new date for taking over the works either as a result of reviewing previous decisions, or as a result of any default by the employer committed after the date of the architect's certificate of non-completion under clause 11.2. The grounds for extension of time are confined in alternative one to employer's default. Alternative two adds the following grounds:

- *Force majeure.*
- Damage due to insured risks.
- War, disorder, and so on.
- Delay by government agency, local authority or statutory undertaker.

If the contractor fails to complete the work by the date for taking over the work, the architect must issue a certificate to that effect, and the contractor must pay liquidated damages at the rate stated in the time schedule or the employer may require the architect to deduct them from amounts otherwise payable on a certificate. If alternative two of clause 11.3 applies, the employer may deduct unliquidated damages from the contractor.

xv)   Partial completion
Clause 13 allows the employer to take over part of the works if the contractor consents. The consequences are as though that part of the works had been taken over.

xvi)   Assignment and sub-letting
Neither party may assign their rights or obligations under the contract, but there are two provisos:
- The contractor may assign his right to receive payment.
- The employer may assign his rights under the contract after taking over of the works.

Clause 9.2 allows the contractor to sub-let with the architect's consent.

Provision is made for what are termed named sub-contractors. They can occur in three ways:
- A person is named in the documents, and the work or goods is priced by the contractor.
- One or a list of persons is inserted in the documents, and the work is covered by a provision sum for which the architect may issue an instruction.
- A provisional sum is inserted in the documents, and the architect issues an instruction naming a sub-contractor.

There is provision for the situation if the contractor either is unable to enter into contract with the sub-contractor, or if the sub-contract is terminated. If a sub-contractor carries out design, the contractor is fully responsible.

xvii)   Employer's licensees
As section 5.2.

xviii)   Instructions
Under the provisions of clause 8.1 the architect may issue instructions regarding the following:
- Removal of defective work.
- Dismissal of incompetent operatives.
- Opening up and testing.
- Changes in working space or hours.
- Change in design, quality or quantity of work.
- Any matter connected with the works.

**5**   Selected contract terms

- In regard to ambiguities, statutory requirements, ground conditions, samples, sub-contractors, employer's licensees, acceleration or postponement, defects liability and antiquities.

The architect may issue instructions until the contractor has discharged his liability for defects after taking over; the contractor must immediately comply with instructions regarding removal of defective work, dismissal, opening up and changes in working space, and so on. Oral instructions may be given in an emergency, but must be confirmed in writing by the architect within five days. The architect may issue a five-day compliance notice under clause 12.4, and the employer may engage others.

xix)  Payment
Straightforward provisions in clauses 16 and 19. Until taking over occurs, the contractor must submit interim applications monthly. The architect must issue his certificate within ten days. The value of work in a certificate must be as at a date no earlier than ten days before certification. Payment must be made by the employer within ten days of a certificate. Unless the employer is a local authority, retention money must be deposited in a separate bank account. Retention is not released until the final certificate. Within 60 days of the expiry of the maintenance period, the contractor must submit his final account together with supporting documentation. The architect must issue the final certificate 60 days after the contractor has submitted his final account with documentation, and returned all drawings. The final certificate, nor any other certificate, has any degree of conclusivity. Fluctuations are dealt with by clause 18 on the basis of ACA indices.

xx)  Variations and their valuation
The contractor must submit written estimates of the value of the instruction, any extension of time, and any damage, loss and/or expense. The architect may agree, otherwise he may instruct the contractor not to comply; instruct him to comply and ascertain a fair and reasonable adjustment of the contract sum together with extension of time and loss and/or expense or refer the matter to the adjudicator. The architect may choose to dispense with estimates when issuing the instruction.

xxi)  Loss and/or expense
Clause 7 stipulates that the contractor may claim damage, loss

**5.10**  ACA 2

and/or expense, except for instructions, by giving notice to the architect immediately an event giving rise to a claim occurs or is likely to occur. He must also submit an estimate of the adjustment required with his next interim application for payment. He must continue to submit estimates as long as the losses continue. The architect may either accept the estimate, or state that he wishes to negotiate. If agreement cannot be reached within 20 days, either party can refer the estimates to the adjudicator.

xxii) Contract sum
The quality and quantity of the work is set out in the contract documents. Adjustment of the contract sum is authorised in 13 different places in the contract.

xxiii) Antiquities
As section 5.2.

xxiv) War
No reference.

xxv) Termination
Either party may terminate the contractor's employment for stipulated reasons:
The employer, after written notice, if the contractor:
- wholly suspends the works without reasonable cause; or
- fails to comply with obligations regarding assignment and sub-letting; or
- fails to proceed regularly and diligently; or
- does not comply with architect's instruction; or
- is otherwise in breach.
Termination may be without notice if the contractor is insolvent.
The contractor, after written notice, if the employer:
- does not pay amounts due; or
- obstructs the issue of a certificate; or
- is otherwise in breach and the contractor is delayed for at least 20 days.
Termination may be without notice if the employer is insolvent.
Whoever terminates, either party can refer the dispute to the adjudicator within 20 days of the default notice. Otherwise, entitlement to terminate is not open to challenge.
Either party if the works are suspended for a period of 60 days due to:
- *force majeure*; or
- loss or damage due to insured risks; or

- war, disorder, etc.

The provisions are to be found in clauses 20, 21 and 22. The consequences of termination involve:

If the employer terminates:

- The contractor must give up possession of the site.
- He is not bound to make further payment until final cost of completion by others is ascertained.
- He may charge the contractor damage, loss and/or expense.
- He may charge the contractor the difference in cost in having others to complete.

If the contractor terminates:

- The contractor must give up possession of the site.
- He must be paid amounts due.
- He must be paid the cost of protecting the works.

If either party terminates, the situation is the same as if the contractor had terminated, but neither party has a claim for damage, loss and/or expense against the other.

xxvi)  Disputes

The procedure for dealing with disputes may be adjudication, arbitration or litigation.

Under the adjudication option, the adjudicator is to decide certain specific disputes as a first stage. If either party is dissatisfied with the decision, reference can be made to arbitration, but the adjudication is in place until taking over the works.

Under the arbitration option, disputes are first to be referred to the architect for his decision, which is to be in place until taking over the works. If either party is dissatisfied, it can be referred to the decision of an arbitrator agreed by the party or in default appointed by the President or Vice-President of the Chartered Institute of Arbitrators.

The litigation option purports to give the courts the same powers to, for example, open up decisions as an arbitrator.

## 5.11
## ASI Building Contract

i)  Type of contract
As section 5.2.

ii)  The contract documents
- specification; and/or

- bills of quantities; and/or
- drawings; and
- any other necessary documents; and
- printed form.

iii) Type of price
As section 5.2.

iv) Provision for architect, and so on
The first recital provides for the insertion of the name of an architect, surveyor or engineer. If not an architect, the description 'architect' used in the conditions is deemed changed to surveyor or engineer as appropriate. There is also provision for the insertion of the name of a quantity surveyor. If any nominated person ceases to act, the employer may nominate another person to whom the contractor does not object.

v) Unusual provisions
None.

vi) Contractor's obligations
Principally contained in clause 1.1 to provide everything necessary for and to carry out and complete the works in accordance with the contract documents and any further information supplied by the architect. The contractor must exercise the skill, care and diligence of a competent and experienced contractor.

vii) Provision of information
Either before or when the contract is signed, the contractor must give the architect a fully priced copy of the bills of quantities or other priced document. The architect must give the contractor a copy of the contract documents, two copies of drawings, specifications, and any further particulars. Clause 2.4 empowers the architect to issue further drawings, and so on necessary to describe the work. The contractor must provide the architect with two copies of his progress chart within three weeks of signing the contract. The contractor must check the drawings and, if he finds a difference, it is to be notified to the architect.

viii) Statutory requirements
As section 5.2.

**5** Selected contract terms

ix) Site personnel
Clause 3.2 stipulates that the contractor must keep a competent site agent on site during working hours. He must also employ adequate skilled staff. The architect is empowered to require the exclusion of any employee from the site. The employer is entitled to employ a clerk or clerks of work who is under the direction of the architect, and who may issue directions which must be confirmed by the architect.

x) Vesting of property
As section 5.2.

xi) Insurance
Clause 8.4 provides for the contractor to indemnify the employer and take out insurance against personal injury and death or damage to property, unless caused by the negligence of the contractor or employer in which case the contractor or employer will be liable. Clause 8.42 requires the contractor to insure against damage to property other than the works where negligence is not involved.

Where new work is involved, the insurance may be taken out by the contractor or employer in joint names against clause 8.61 perils. In the case of existing buildings, insurance is to be taken out by the employer in respect of the existing building and the new part of the works. There are provisions in respect of the production of evidence of insurance and the power to insure by the other party in case of default. The contractor is obliged to restore damaged work in every case, but in the case of new work, he is entitled to receive only the amount of insurance payment. In the case of an existing building, he is entitled to be paid as though the reinstatement was a variation.

xii) Possession of the site
Possession of the site is dealt with by clause 4.1. The employer must give possession of and access to the site on the date stated in the contract. The contractor must proceed diligently and expeditiously to completion.

xiii) Completion, defects liability
Clause 4.1 makes clear that the contractor must complete the works on or before the contract completion date. The date of practical completion is to be discussed with and approved by the architect. Presumably the contractor will discuss. Among other things, the defects liability period then starts and the contractor

**5.11** ASI Building Contract

is responsible for rectifying any defects which occur during the period; the architect must issue a list of outstanding defects to the contractor at or soon after the end of the period.

xiv) Extensions of time, damages for delay
The contractor must notify the architect promptly when delay becomes apparent. He must state the reasons and give his estimate of the delay beyond completion date.

The contractor, by clause 4.42, is required to claim an extension of time and produce a reasoned case clearly related to one or more of the causes of delay. At practical completion and no later than four weeks after, he must submit a summary case for the total extension of time he wishes to claim. The architect must consider any claim for extension of time submitted by the contractor if resulting from a variation order issued after the date of practical completion. The architect must grant appropriate extensions of time, but he may defer his final decision until after practical completion. The causes of delay may be summarised as follows:

- Exceptionally adverse weather.
- Significant delay by nominated sub-contractors.
- Significant delays by statutory undertakers.
- Inability to obtain labour or materials.
- Exercise of statutory power.
- Civil commotion, strikes, and so on.
- Damage due to clause 8.6 perils.
- Frustration caused by the employer over access.
- Employer's men or materials.
- Variation orders.
- Opening up and testing.
- Antiquities.
- *Force majeure.*

If the contractor fails to complete the works by the contract or extended completion date, the contractor must pay the employer liquidated damages at the rate set out in the contract or the period of delay assessed and confirmed in writing by the architect. The employer may recover the money as a debt.

xv) Partial completion
The provisions are obscure. The employer may require to take possession of part of the work or agree it with the contractor. The contractor must submit a written statement of outstanding work and also a list of suggested responsibilities involved, such as insurance. Liquidated damages must be reduced in proportion to the value of the part handed over.

5   Selected contract terms

xvi)  Assignment and sub-letting
Neither party may assign the contract without consent. The contractor may sub-let, but must give the architect a list of proposed sub-contractors whom the architect may reject. Excessive sub-letting or non-declaration is said to allow the employer to determine the contractor's employment, but no details are given.

There architect may nominate specialist firms to carry out work. There are few other provisions except for direct payment in certain circumstances.

xvii)  Employer's licensees
If the employer wishes to do work or supply only items, the contractor must permit it if defined in the specification. If not so defined, the contractor's consent is required.

xviii)  Instructions
Under clause 2.3, the architect may issue instruction and the contractor must comply forthwith. The architect may issue a 14 day compliance notice and the employer may engage others. Oral instructions must be confirmed by the contractor or the architect. By what must be an unenforceable clause 2.32, the contractor is liable to pay damages at the rate in the contract for any delay period between the architect's instruction and the restarting of the work unless the contract is finished on time.

xix)  Payment
Certificates are to be issued monthly or as stated in A5.5 until practical completion. Payment must be made by the employer within 14 days of a certificate issued by the architect. Certificates and valuations are to be prepared by the quantity surveyor, if any. Otherwise the contractor must submit his application 14 days before a certificate is due, properly supported by documentation for checking by the architect. Unless the employer is a government department or a local authority, retention money is to be deposited in a separate bank account. Retention must be released half at practical completion and the remainder at the issue of the final certificate. The contractor must submit before or soon after practical completion all the documentation for calculation of the final account. The quantity surveyor and the contractor or (if there is no quantity surveyor) the contractor will prepare the final account and send it to the architect for approval. Checking must be completed within the

**5.11**   ASI Building Contract

period of account noted in Article 5.8 from satisfactory rectification of defects, the end of the defects liability period, or the receipt by the architect of all the account particulars, whichever is later. The final certificate must be issued as soon as practicable after the defects have been made good satisfactorily. Alternatively, it must be issued at the end of the defects liability period and after completion of all outstanding items of work to the architect's satisfaction and his approval of the final account. No certificate is to be taken as conclusive evidence that work, materials or goods are in accordance with the contract.

Fluctuations are the subject of optional clauses 7.3, 7.4 or 7.5 which allow fluctuations for statutory increases, labour and materials, or adjustment by formula rules respectively.

xx) Variations and their valuation

The rules for variations are set out in clause 7. The architect must stipulate the basis of costing at the time of issuing the variation order. The valuation is to be on the basis of the prices in the bills of quantities, priced specification or schedule of rates or at rates approved by the architect before work proceeds if work is not included in the priced document but is capable of measurement or on a quotation before work proceeds or by daywork.

xxi) Loss and/or expense

The contractor may claim direct loss and/or expense if regular progress has been disrupted due to any of the following causes:

- Discrepancies between documents.
- Frustration by the employer over access to the site.
- Employer's men or materials.
- Variations.
- Postponement.
- Late information.
- Opening up and testing.

The contractor must make written application as soon as loss and/or expense becomes apparent together with relevant particulars. He must then submit a quantified claim in duplicate and a reasoned case in support. If several claims are made at, but no later than four weeks after, practical completion, the contractor must submit to the architect a summary case in duplicate. The architect is to decide if the claim is valid and, together with the quantity surveyor if appointed, assess the amount. Nominated sub-contractors' claims are also to be submitted in the same way.

**5**   Selected contract terms

xxii) Contract sum
The quality and quantity of the materials, goods and workmanship is to be the best of their respective kinds in accordance with the drawings and specification and bills of quantities.

xxiii) Antiquities
As section 5.2.

xxiv) War
As section 5.2.

xxv) Termination
Either party may determine the contractor's employment for stipulated reasons:
The employer, after two sets of written notices, if the contractor:
- Fails to proceed regularly and diligently.
- Wholly suspends the works without cause.
- Refuses to replace defective work or to comply with architect's instructions.

In the case of insolvency, determination is automatic.
The contractor if:
- The employer does not pay the amount due after notice.
- The employer delays the work for four continuous weeks.
- The employer persistently interrupts and delays the work.
- The employer becomes insolvent.
- Reasons beyond the contractor's control delay the work for four continuous weeks.
- Damage due to insured risks or other reasonable cause delay the works for three consecutive months.

The provisions are to be found in clauses 9.1 and 9.2. The consequences of determination involve:
If the employer determines:
- The contractor must give up possession of the site.
- The employer may pay others to complete the work.
- He may use contractor's equipment and/or require its removal.
- He may charge the contractor loss and/or damage and the difference in cost of having others to complete. He is liable for work done but need not pay the contractor, if at all, until after completion and the total cost has been verified.
If the contractor determines:
- He must be paid the value of work done.

**5.11**  ASI Building Contract

- He is entitled to any loss and/or damage warranted by the determination.
- He must remove his equipment.
- The employer must pay for all goods legally due to be paid for by the contractor.

xxvi) Disputes

The procedure is to be arbitration. Clause 10 applies. Any dispute must first be put to the architect. Either party may refer disputes to arbitration. If there is no agreement on the arbitrator, the President of the Architects and Surveyors Institute can be asked to nominate. If there is a related arbitration involving a sub-contractor or supplier, the two references can be joined. The arbitrator is given wider powers than the courts to review directions, instructions or certificates. Except by agreement, arbitration cannot be opened until after practical completion, termination or abandonment or the work except in specified circumstances. There is provision for arbitration to be carried out under a shortened procedure.

## 5.12
## ASI Small Works Contract

i) Type of contract

This is a traditional form of contract which caters for the situation where the architect prepares the production information and the contractor tenders to carry out the work without any design responsibility. The entire scope and nature of the work should be known at the time of tender, although there is provision for variations in the work after commencement on site.

ii) The contract documents
- printed form; and
- contract drawings; and
- bills of quantities (if supplement used); or
- specification; and/or
- schedule of works.

iii) Type of price
As section 5.2.

iv) Provision for architect, etc.
The first recital provides for the insertion of the name of the

**5**   Selected contract terms

architect, surveyor or engineer. If not an architect, the description 'architect' used in the conditions is deemed changed to surveyor or engineer as appropriate. If a nominated person ceases to act, the employer may nominate another person to whom the contractor does not object. If the supplementary conditions are used, the name of a quantity surveyor may be inserted in addition to the architect, surveyor or engineer.

v) Unusual provisions
None.

vi) Contractor's obligations
Principally contained in clause 1.1 to provide everything necessary for and to carry out and complete the works in accordance with the contract documents and any further information supplied by the architect.

vii) Provision of information
Either before or when the contract is signed, the contractor must give the architect a full schedule of rates and a priced specification or schedule of works. If the supplementary conditions are used, the contractor will hand over a copy of the priced bills of quantities instead. The architect must give the contractor a copy of the contract documents, two copies of drawings and specification or schedule of works (or bills of quantities). Clause 2.4 empowers the architect to issue further drawings and particulars to describe the work. The contractor is not expressly required to check the drawings, but he must notify the architect of any differences. There is no provision for a progress chart to be provided by the contractor.

viii) Statutory requirements
Clause 1.3 states that the contractor shall comply with all legal and statutory requirements and pay all fees which will be set against the provisional sum or added to the contract sum. Before making any changes after inspection by an authority, the contractor must apply to the architect for instructions, if 'warranted' a variation order must be issued. There is no provision for emergency compliance.

ix) Site personnel
As section 5.11.

**5.12** ASI Small Works Contract

x) Vesting of property
Clause 6.34 states that when goods and materials are 'certified' they become the property of the employer, the contractor remains liable for loss or damage.

xi) Insurance
As section 5.11, but: Indemnities in respect of personal injury and death or damage to property have no exclusion in respect of employer's negligence, and there is no express provision for the contractor to maintain any insurance cover beyond practical completion.

xii) Possession of the site
The contractor is to conform with stated dates when work may commence and shall be completed. He must proceed diligently and expeditiously.

xiii) Completion, defects liability
Clause 4.1 makes clear that the contractor must compete by the date for completion. The date for practical completion is to be approved by the architect. The defects liability period then starts and the contractor is responsible for rectifying any defects which occur during the period, and the architect must issue a list of outstanding defects to the contractor at the end of the period.

xiv) Extensions of time, damages for delay
The contractor must notify the architect promptly when delay becomes apparent. He must state the reasons and give his estimate of the delay beyond completion date. The architect must consider any notice and the case submitted by the contractor, and in his absolute discretion grant an appropriate extension of time if warranted by circumstances. It is extremely doubtful that this clause forms an effective means of extending the contract period for delays attributable to the employer. There is no list of causes of delay. If the contractor fails to complete the work by the completion date or any extended date, the contractor shall pay liquidated damages for the period of delay certified by the architect.

xv) Partial completion
No provisions.

xvi) Assignment and sub-letting
As section 5.11 except that only the contractor is prohibited from assigning the contract.

**5** Selected contract terms

xvii)   Employer's licensees
        As section 5.11, but somewhat shorter.

xviii)  Instructions
        As section 5.11.

xix)    Payment
        Interim payments will be at monthly intervals. Payment must be made by the employer within 14 days of the date of issue of the certificate. The contractor must apply to the architect with a statement in suitable detail 14 days before the issue of a certificate is due. If the supplementary conditions are used, the quantity surveyor will do the valuations. Retention money must be deposited in a separate bank account. Retention money must be released, half at practical completion, and the rest at the issue of the final certificate. The contractor must submit at or soon after practical completion his final account and all information needed for the architect to approve and certify. If the supplementary conditions are used, the quantity surveyor will produce the final account valuation from information supplied from the contractor. The architect must issue the final certificate after proper completion of the work and defects, and his approval of the final account adjustments. No certificate is to be taken as conclusive that work, materials or goods to which it relates are in accordance with the contract. Fluctuations are the subject of clauses 7.3 or 7.4, which allow for statutory increases or labour and materials respectively.

xx)     Variations and valuations
        Rules are set out in clause 7. The architect must stipulate the basis of costing at the time of issuing the variation order. Valuation is to be on the basis of prices in the priced specification or schedule of rates, or at rates approved by the architect before work commences if the work is capable of measurement, or on quotation, or by daywork. Where the supplementary conditions are used, all measuring is to be carried out by the quantity surveyor.

xxi)    Loss and/or expense
        Claims by the contractor or nominated sub-contractor for direct loss and/or expense may be submitted in writing together with appropriate supporting information not later than four weeks from the date of practical completion for the architect to consider and certify any amount warranted.

**5.12**   ASI Small Works Contract

xxii)  Contract sum
The quality and quantity of the materials, goods and workmanship is to be the best of their respective kinds in accordance with the drawings and specification or schedules of work.

xxiii)  Antiquities
No provisions.

xxiv)  War
As section 5.2.

xxv)  Termination
Either party may determine the contractor's employment for stipulated reasons:
The employer, without prior notice, if the contractor:
* Fails to proceed with reasonable diligence.
* Wholly suspends the work without cause
* Refuses or neglects to comply with architect's instructions for 14 clear days after notice.
* Becomes insolvent.
The contractor if:
* The employer does not pay amount due after notice.
* The employer delays the work for four continuous weeks.
* The employer becomes insolvent.
The provisions are to be found in clauses 9.1 and 9.2. The consequences of determination involve:
If the employer determines:
* The contractor must give up the works.
* The employer may pay others to complete the work.
* He may use the contractor's equipment and/or require its removal.
* He may charge the contractor loss and/or damage and the difference in cost in having others to complete. He is liable for work done, but need not pay the contractor until after completion and the total cost has been verified. There may be a debt due to the employer.
If the contractor determines:
* He must be paid the value of work done.
* He is entitled to any loss and/or damage warranted by the determination.

xxvi)  Disputes
The procedure is to be arbitration. Clause 10 applies. Any dispute

**5**  Selected contract terms

is to be put first to the architect for his decision. Any unresolved dispute may be put to a person agreed between the parties or nominated by the President of the Architects and Surveyors Institute. The arbitrator is given no special powers.

## 5.13
## ASI Minor Works Contract

i)   Type of contract
     As section 5.12.

ii)  The contract documents
     * printed form; and
     * drawings; and/or
     * specification; and/or
     * schedule of work.

iii) Type of price
     Lump sum. In principle, this is a fixed price contract, although the contract provisions soften this effect as far as the contractor is concerned, for example by providing for the valuation of variations.

iv)  Provision for architect and so on
     As section 5.12, except that there is no provision for use of supplementary conditions and no quantity surveyor. Whoever is named in the recital (architect, surveyor or engineer), he is referred to throughout the remainder of the contract as 'the adviser'.

v)   Unusual provisions
     None.

vi)  Contractor's obligations
     As section 5.12.

vii) Provision of information
     The adviser 'will' issue further information and instructions as necessary, confirmed in writing.

viii) Statutory requirements
     Clause 1.3 states that the contractor comply with all legal and statutory requirements, serve all notices and pay all fees.

ix) Site personnel
The contractor must keep a competent person in charge during working hours who is empowered to discuss the work with and take the adviser's instructions.

x) Vesting of property
No provisions.

xi) Insurance
Clause 8.4 provides for the contractor to indemnify the employer and take out insurance against personal injury and death or damage to property. There is no exclusion in respect of employer's negligence. Clause 8.42 requires the contractor to insure against damage to property other than the works where negligence is not involved.

Where new work is involved, the insurance must be taken out by the contractor in joint names against specific listed perils. In the case of existing buildings, insurance is to be taken out by the employer for the existing and new work. There are provisions for the production of evidence of insurance in the absence of which the other party has power to insure and claim or deduct premiums as appropriate. The contractor is obliged to restore damaged work in each case, but in the case of new work he is entitled to receive only the amount of insurance payment. In the case of existing buildings, he is entitled to be paid as though the reinstatement was a variation.

xii) Possession of the site
Dates are stated when work may commence and must be completed. The contractor must proceed diligently and expeditiously.

xiii) Completion, defects liability
As section 5.12.

xiv) Extensions of time, damages for delay
The contractor must notify the adviser promptly if it becomes apparent that the works will not be completed by the completion date. The adviser must 'in his absolute discretion' grant an extension of time if the circumstances warrant it. It is doubtful that this clause will be effective in empowering the adviser to extend the period when delays are attributable to the employer. It is not clear in what circumstances the contractor is to pay liquidated damages for the period certified by the adviser.

**5** Selected contract terms

xv)   Partial completion
No provisions.

xvi)   Assignment and sub-letting
The only provision prohibits the contractor from assigning the contract or sub-letting any part of the work without the adviser's written consent.

xvii)   Employer's licensees
No provisions.

xviii)   Instructions
Clause 2.1 empowers the adviser to issue further instructions as necessary. There are no further provisions.

xix)   Payment
There are alternative clauses, 6.1 or 6.2, depending on whether payment is to be in one sum after proper completion of the work and defects and certification of the contractor's account, or from time to time at the discretion of the adviser respectively. All payments are to be made under certificates of the adviser within 14 days of the employer receiving the certificate. The retention percentage is to be inserted. It is to be held in trust, but there are no express provisions for it to be held in a separate bank account, or for its release before the final certificate. The contractor is to supply all necessary information to enable the adviser to approve and certify the appropriate amount. After proper completion of the work and defects, the adviser will issue the final certificate. No certificate must be taken as conclusive evidence that the work, materials or goods to which it relates are in accordance with the contract. Fluctuations are allowable only on the basis of statutory increases.

xx)   Variations and valuations
Rules are set out in clause 7. The adviser must stipulate the method of costing at the time of issuing the variation order. Valuation is to be on the basis of prices in the schedule of work or schedule of rates, or at rates approved by the adviser before work proceeds if the work is capable of measurement, or on quotation, or by daywork.

xxi)   Loss and/or expense
There appears to be no provision for the contractor to recover loss and/or expense under the terms of the contract. Clause 10.1

**5.13**   ASI Minor Works Contract

may be intended to serve this purpose, but it is doubtful whether it is effective.

xxii) Contract sum
As section 5.12.

xxiii) Antiquities
No provisions.

xxiv) War
No provisions.

xxv) Termination
The grounds for termination are generally as section 5.12, but the consequences are restricted. If the employer terminates, he has no right to use the original contractor's equipment to finish the works, nor may he deduct any loss and/or damage he has suffered. If the contractor terminates, there is no express provision entitling him to loss and/or damage suffered.

xxvi) Disputes
As section 5.12.

# 6 Key provisions compared

**6.1**
**Introduction**

Although contracts are written so as to cover all situations which are likely to arise within their field of use, the provisions are not of equal weight. Some are less important because the chances of operation are fairly remote. Among this type of clause is JCT 80 clause 32 Outbreak of Hostilities. Other clauses must be given less weight because without them the contract would still be capable of operating reasonably well either without the clause at all or because an implied term would fill the gap. Into this category are clauses dealing with person-in-charge, clerk of works, access for the architect to the works and so on.

The point is not that these are not perfectly good clauses, but that in deciding upon the most suitable form of contract for a particular situation, there are other more important clauses which must be taken into account. After all, if there is no clause dealing with the provision of a clerk of works, it is not too difficult to insert one. If, however, the payments clause is defective, it is a serious flaw in the contract.

Which are the most important clauses is, of course, a subjective matter to some extent and the parameters will certainly vary with the project under consideration. This chapter considers some alternative clauses in the standard forms under discussion. The parameters are reasonably widely drawn around the critical provisions as follows:

- Contract documents.
- Type of price.
- Contractor's obligations.
- Provision of information.
- Insurance.
- Extension of time, damages for delay.
- Assignment and sub-letting.
- Payment.
- Loss and/or expense.
- Termination.
- Disputes.

**6.2**
**Contract documents**

When two parties enter into a contract which they put into writing, they are assumed in law to have committed to paper all the terms they wish to govern that contract. For example, neither of the parties can bring oral evidence to add or subtract or in any way vary the written terms. Moreover, the courts will, in general, exclude all other pre-contract exchanges of letters.

**6.2   Contract documents**

The exceptions to this are:
- If the court requires assistance regarding the meaning of a foreign language or trade terms.
- To show evidence of fraud or illegality.
- To show that there is a collateral contract.
- To show that the contract has been rescinded.
- To show that there was a precondition to a binding contract.
- To resolve ambiguities.

The contract documents are, therefore, of primary importance because they are the written evidence of the contract gathered together by the parties. One of the advantages of a standard form over a simple exchange of letters is that the extent of the contract documents is clearly identifiable. In the case of an exchange of letters, the precise extent of the contract documents may itself be the subject of dispute.

Take, for example, the situation where an architect on behalf of his client writes to a contractor requesting a quotation for carrying out some work shown on enclosed drawings. The contractor may reply with a quotation which does not cover all the work or he may give a price on the understanding that certain materials are substituted. Some standard conditions may be mentioned by one or other as being relevant. The architect may 'accept', subject to agreeing a number of items. The contractor may reply agreeing some, but not others, and so on. The correspondence in such cases can, and usually does, become quite voluminous. At some point, presumably, the contractor will proceed to carry out the work. By this time, the question may be: which work and on what terms? The problem of sorting out which letters are part of the contract or which parts of which letters, or sometimes deciding if there is a contract at all, is often a matter for the court; very expensive it is too. It is, therefore, crucial that the contract documents:
- contain all the terms the parties wish to apply; and
- are clearly identified.

Documents other than the printed form are normally identified by being endorsed with some such sentence as: 'This is one of the contract documents referred to in the contract dated...'. The parties then sign and date them at the same time as the printed form. In the case of a bound document such as a specification, it is usually sufficient to endorse and sign it once only on the cover. Every separate drawing sheet should be endorsed and signed.

In the case of the standard forms under consideration, the printed form itself is always one of the contract documents.

**6   Key provisions compared**

Every standard form has provisions to indicate the extent of the other documents. In general, a good principle to follow is that the documents sent to the contractor and on which he bases his tender become the contract documents together with the printed form. The reason for this is that when the contractor puts in a tender, what he is offering to do for the price is the works described and/or drawn on the information he has been sent. As far as possible, everything which you wish to apply to the contract should be notified to the contractor before tendering and you should make sure that his tender includes everything. For example, if you do not ensure that a suitable reference is included in the contract documents, you cannot expect the contractor to finish work at noon on Thursdays no matter how important it may be.

If you wish him to finish work early on a particular day, you must tell him when you invite tenders. In that way, when your client accepts the tender, finishing early becomes a term of the contract. If your project has gone out to tender on the basis of a sketch drawing and a two-page description, do not be surprised if the contractor points out that all those excellent details you subsequently produce will cost extra because he has allowed for very basic detailing in his price. What you do not ask for you do not get. This is very much the kind of situation which can arise under short forms such as MW 80, ASI SW and ASI MW if care is not taken to tie up all the loose ends. The problem is that the forms will operate simply on the basis of drawings plus printed form, but the drawings must comprehensively state what is required. All standard forms provide for drawings as part of the contract documents. If the drawings are to stand alone, they must be detailed as has already been explained. If other documents are to be provided, the drawings can, and indeed probably should, be less detailed and the missing information can be provided in another form.

JCT 80 With Quantities and With Approximate Quantities, IFC 84, ACA 2 and the ASI form allow the use of bills of quantities. ASI SW allows for the use of bills of quantities if the supplementary conditions are used. While the JCT forms make specific provision for the method of measurement to be adopted and the treatment of errors in the bills, ACA 2 and ASI refer only to correction of the bills. Clearly, it is essential to establish how the bills have been prepared because otherwise there is no objective yardstick for deciding how much work is included in the contractor's price and variations become very difficult to value. It is possible that, in the absence of an express term, the courts would be willing to imply a term that the bills have been

**6.2**   Contract documents

prepared in accordance with the current Standard Method of Measurement, but that itself would spell disaster if the bills had been taken off in some other way.

An alternative to bills of quantities is the specification. It is offered by JCT 80 Without Quantities, IFC 84, MW 80, Fixed Fee Form of Prime Cost, JCT 87, ACA 2, ASI, ASI SW and ASI MW. In some forms, but not JCT 80 With Quantities, the specification may be used with bills of quantities. Where the specification is a contract document it is sometimes priced by the contractor. This is the case with JCT 80 Without Quantities, IFC 84, MW 80 and ASI MW. It then becomes the priced document used for the valuation of variations. It should be noted that only in the case of JCT 80 Without Quantities does the priced specification become a contract document. Care must be taken because it is common to find that quantities of some, but not all, items have been included in the specification. The contractor may well literally price the specification as if it was exhaustive of the whole of the work with scant reference to the drawings. The effect of that will depend on the form of contract.

Under the provisions of MW 80, ACA 2, ASI, ASI SW and ASI MW the position appears to be that the contractor's lump sum total represents his price for carrying out the work whether in the specification or on the drawings. He cannot expect a variation because something is included in one document, but not the other. The documents are indeed intended to supplement each other. JCT 80 Without Quantities and IFC 84, however, include provisions which enable the contractor clearly to identify what he is to price. This is accomplished by clauses 14.1 and 1.2 respectively which, though complex, present a set of rules for deciding just what is included in the contractor's price.

As an alternative, JCT 80 Without Quantities, IFC 84, MW 80, the BPF version of ACA 2, ASI SW and ASI MW refer to a schedule of work (called simply 'schedules' in MW 80 and 'schedule of activity' in ACA/BPF). Just exactly what is contained in the schedule of work will depend upon you (except in regard to ACA/BPF, the manual to which lays down clear guidance on the form and content of the schedule of activities). There are some professionals who consider such a schedule an improvement on bills of quantities, because the work and materials are not divided artificially, but into work packages in a logical way. These schedules can be priced to form a basis for the valuation of variations or a separate schedule of rates and prices can be submitted. This is not always a contract document (in the case of MW 80 for example).

**6** Key provisions compared

**Table 6.1**
Contract documents

| Document | JCT 80 With Quantities | JCT 80 With Approximate Quantities | JCT 80 Without Quantities | IFC 84 Intermediate Form | MW80 Minor Works Form | JCT 81 With Contractor's Design | JCT Fixed Fee Form | JCT 87 Management Contract | ACA 2 | ASI | ASI SW | ASI MW |
|---|---|---|---|---|---|---|---|---|---|---|---|---|
| Printed form of contract | ● | ● | ● | ● | ● | ● | ● | ● | ● | ● | ● | ● |
| Drawings | ● | ● | ● | ● | ● | ● | ● | ● | ● | ● | ● | ● |
| Project drawings | – | – | – | – | – | – | – | ● | – | – | – | – |
| Project specification | – | – | – | – | – | – | – | ● | – | – | – | – |
| Specification | – | – | – | – | ● | – | ● | – | ● | ● | ● | ● |
| Priced specification | – | – | ● | ● | – | – | – | – | – | – | – | – |
| Bills of quantities | ● | – | – | ● | – | – | – | – | ● | ● | ● | – |
| Bills of approximate quantities | – | ● | – | – | – | – | – | – | – | – | – | – |
| Schedules of rates | – | – | – | – | – | – | – | – | ● | – | – | – |
| Schedules of work | – | – | – | – | – | – | – | – | – | – | ● | ● |
| Priced schedules of work | – | – | ● | ● | – | – | – | – | – | – | – | – |
| Schedules | – | – | – | – | ● | – | – | – | – | – | – | – |
| Schedules 1–5 inclusive | – | – | – | – | – | – | – | ● | – | – | – | – |
| NAM/T | – | – | – | ● | – | – | – | – | – | – | – | – |
| Formula rules schedule | – | – | ● | – | – | – | – | – | – | – | – | – |
| Time schedule | – | – | – | – | – | – | – | – | ● | – | – | – |
| Employer's requirements | – | – | – | – | – | ● | – | – | – | – | – | – |
| Contractor's proposals | – | – | – | – | – | ● | – | – | – | – | – | – |
| Contract sum analysis | – | – | – | – | – | ● | – | – | – | – | – | – |
| Contract cost plan | – | – | – | – | – | – | – | ● | – | – | – | – |
| Any other necessary documents | – | – | – | – | – | – | – | – | – | ● | – | – |

JCT 80 Without Quantities and IFC 84 somewhat curiously provides (in alternative B of the second recital) for the contractor to submit his price as a lump sum, for the contract documents to be the printed form, drawings and specification and for the contractor to supply the employer with a contract sum analysis or a schedule of rates. Neither of these documents are to be

**6.2**  Contract documents

contract documents although, in that alternative, one or the other will form the basis for valuation.

Certain forms of contract have particular contract documents to suit their purposes. JCT 81 has the Employer's Requirements, the Contractor's Proposals and the Contract Sum Analysis. The Employer's Requirements may vary in size and complexity from the briefest description to outline drawings supported by a thorough performance specification. It is intended to elicit a response from the contractor in the form of his proposals. Just how extensive they will be largely depends upon the form in which they have been requested. Normally, you could expect to see them in the form of reasonably detailed design drawings, together with a comprehensive specification.

JCT 87 requires a project drawing and a project specification. These documents are not likely to be developed at the point when the management contractor becomes involved. In addition, an agreed cost plan and a set of schedules based on schedules in the printed form are included in the documents. Since the idea of the contract is that the management contractor will enter into a contract before the project is finalised, a different set of criteria from the usual must be employed when considering whether the contract documents are appropriate. Table 6.1 compares contract documents for various forms of contract.

**6.3**
**Type of price**

The Fixed Fee Form of Prime Cost and JCT 87 are not forms of contract which produce a lump sum price. They are both based on a fixed fee plus the prime cost of the work. To that extent, therefore, it is less important that the documents tie up the work to be carried out for the price. Indeed, the essence of both these contracts is that, for various reasons, the work will be adjusted during the currency of the contract. The same comments might be made, to a lesser extent, in relation to JCT 80 With Approximate Quantities. In that case, the work carried out is completely remeasured as it is executed and the total amount of the remeasure becomes the ascertained final sum.

JCT 80, IFC 84, MW 80, JCT 81, ACA 2, ASI, ASI SW and ASI MW forms are all on a lump sum basis. In principle, that means that they are fixed price contracts, which means that the price the contractor tenders for carrying out the work is the payment he is entitled to receive at the end of the contract. In practice, each contract has provision for fluctuations to varying degrees and for the valuation of variations ordered by the architect or, in the case of JCT 81, the employer.

**6** Key provisions compared

MW 80, ASI MW, JCT 80 Without Quantities, IFC 84 used with specification and ACA 2 used with specification are very much more fixed priced than forms which incorporate quantities. In the latter instances, the employer in effect warrants to the contractor that the bills have been prepared accurately and thus if there is any under-measurement or error, it is adjusted and treated as a variation for payment. In the former instances, it is for the contractor to ensure that his price includes everything contained in the specification and drawings read together. The opportunities for additional payment are, therefore, very much less.

**6.4**
**Contractor's obligations**

Contractor's obligations are provided for near the beginning of each form of contract. If it is possible to point to one clause in the contract as the most important, the clause relating to contractor's obligations must be the one. It concisely states what the contractor must do as his part of the contract. It is very much the clause to which the architect can return again and again to get at the fundamental intent of the contract.
All versions of JCT 80, IFC 84 and the Fixed Fee form set out the contractor's obligations in identical or very similar wording. It is in two parts:

- The contractor must carry out and complete the works in accordance with the contract documents.
- If the architect has reserved to himself the approval of any materials or workmanship, he must give or withhold his approval reasonably.

The contractor does not have a dual obligation under this clause, however, because the second part is a proviso to the first part. The first part is a model of clarity and the only problems which can occur are if the contract documents are not quite as clear as they might be. The second part, however, is much more difficult. Specifications and bills of quantities are commonly littered with expressions such as 'or equal approved' or 'unless expressly stated otherwise all materials are to be the approval of the architect' or 'or other approved' or 'to the architect's satisfaction', and so on. The final certificate is stated to be conclusive in all these instances that the architect is satisfied. This is the case whether or not he has inspected the item of workmanship or the material in question.

MW 80 has a very similar provision, but the final certificate is not expressed to be conclusive about anything. JCT 81 is also expressed in similar terms, but the contractor is to complete the design including the selection of specification in so far as not described in the Employer's Requirements or the Contractor's Proposals. His design responsibility in general is stated to be the same as that of an architect. He is not required to warrant fitness for purpose unless dwellings are involved when the provisions of the Defective Premises Act 1972 take effect.

The contractor's obligations under the provisions of JCT 87 are set down in some detail. They relate to his co-operation with the professional team during the pre-construction stage and the management of the works so as to ensure that they are properly executed during the construction stage in accordance with the project specification and the works contracts. There is a similar proviso to the one noted earlier that matters left to the architect's satisfaction are to be to his reasonable satisfaction and the final certificate is again conclusive on this point. The contractor must provide the facilities set out in the fifth schedule and he is liable to the employer for any breach. This last obligation, however, is much tempered by the provisions of clause 3.21 which effectively prevents the employer from recovering from the contractor unless he has been able to recover from the works contractors.

ACA 2 sets out the contractor's obligations very comprehensively. Besides the obligation, similar to the JCT series, to carry out the works in accordance with the contract documents, the contractor is expressly required to use the skill and care of a contractor qualified and experienced in carrying out work of a similar size. This is something which would be implied. By an optional clause, the contractor can be given a design obligation which extends in this contract to fitness for purpose unlike the JCT 81 equivalent. The ASI provision is similar except that there is no design option and the contractor is required to 'provide everything necessary'. This expression is probably enough to cover items which may be inadvertently omitted, but which everyone knows are intended to be part of the contractor's work. The ASI SW and ASI MW versions also included the expression to similar effect, but there is no reference and no need to refer to the standard of the contractor's skill, care and diligence.

**6   Key provisions compared**

**6.5**
**Provision of information**

In general the provision of information is either the responsibility of the architect or the contractor. Except under JCT 81 where the employer acts, the architect must ensure that the contractor receives a set of contract documents. Unless the contractor is responsible for design, a duty is placed on the architect to provide such further information as reasonably necessary to explain and amplify the contract drawings or to enable the contractor to carry out and complete the work in accordance with the contract. It should be noted that this duty is quite irrespective of whether the contractor specifically applies for the information.

**Table 6.2**
Provision
of information

|  | JCT 80 With Quantities | JCT 80 With Approximate Quantities | JCT 80 Without Quantities | IFC 84 Intermediate Form | MW80 Minor Works Form | JCT 81 With Contractor's Design | JCT Fixed Fee Form | JCT 87 Management Contract | ACA 2 | ASI | ASI SW | ASI MW |
|---|---|---|---|---|---|---|---|---|---|---|---|---|
| Contract documents from architect | ● | ● | ● | ● | – | ● | – | ● | – | ● | ● | – |
| Contract drawings from architect | ● | ● | ● | ● | – | – | – | – | – | ● | ● | – |
| Contract bills from architect | ● | ● | – | ● | – | – | – | – | – | ● | – | – |
| Contract spec. from architect | – | – | ● | ● | – | – | – | – | – | ● | ● | – |
| More information from architect | ● | ● | ● | ● | ● | – | ● | ● | ● | ● | ● | ● |
| More information from contractor | – | – | – | – | – | ● | – | – | ● | – | – | – |
| Programme from contractor | ● | ● | ● | – | – | – | – | – | – | ● | – | – |
| Discrepancies between documents | ● | ● | ● | ● | ● | – | – | – | – | ● | ● | – |
| Discrepancies in documents | – | – | – | – | – | ● | – | – | – | – | – | – |
| Prohibition on use of documents | ● | ● | ● | ● | – | ● | ● | ● | ● | ● | ● | – |
| Prohibition on use of rates | ● | ● | ● | ● | – | ● | ● | ● | ● | ● | ● | – |
| Errors in bills | ● | ● | – | ● | – | – | – | – | – | ● | – | – |
| Bills do not override printed form | ● | ● | – | ● | – | – | – | – | – | – | – | – |
| Spec. does not override printed form | – | – | ● | ● | ● | – | – | – | – | – | – | – |
| Employer's requirements etc. do not override printed form | – | – | – | – | – | ● | – | – | – | – | – | – |
| Printed form prevails over all documents | – | – | – | – | – | – | – | – | ● | – | – | – |

6.5 Provision of information

The ASI and ASI SW forms empower the architect to issue further information, but do not place an obligation upon him. JCT 81 envisages that the contractor will provide whatever drawings and other constructional information he requires and he must provide the employer with two copies of each. ACA 2, by means of an optional clause 2 provides for the architect to provide all necessary information or for the contractor to provide all or part of it. The responsibility for preparing further information and the dates by which it must be ready is set out in the Time Schedule.

JCT 80 With Quantities, JCT 80 Without Quantities and JCT 80 With Approximate Quantities provide for the contractor to supply the architect with two copies of his master programme and to update it within 14 days of every extension of time decision. The ASI form requires the contractor to provide two copies of the detailed progress chart. The chart must be revised as necessary and show actual progress on a weekly basis. After extension of time or if revisions are necessary, the contractor must send the architect updated copies.

With the exception of MW 80 and ASI MW, every form forbids the use of information prepared for the works for any other purpose and the divulging of any of the contractor's rates and prices by the employer or architect. JCT 87 alone extends this prohibition to the professional team as a whole. It is in any event an implied obligation. The provisions are compared in Table 6.2.

**6.6 Insurance**

JCT insurance provisions were revised in 1986. JCT 80 With Quantities, JCT 80 Without Quantities, JCT 80 With Approximate Quantities and IFC 84 have identical provisions (see section5.2 (xi)). JCT 81 insurance provisions are identical and it is worth noting that there is no provision in the contract for indemnity insurance in respect of the contractor's design responsibility. There is, of course, nothing to prevent a term to that effect being inserted.

JCT 87 has very similar provisions, but there is no option for the employer to insure new work. There is no provision for the employer to take out insurance if the contractor defaults and is entitled to be paid for restoration work as though it is a change variation whether or not the contractor is responsible for insuring. This is consistent with the general philosophy of this form; that it is relatively low risk for the contractor.

**6** Key provisions compared

ASI SW has provisions which generally follow the provisions in JCT 80 except that they are much shorter and there is only one type of insurance which approximates the JCT 80 'specified perils'. There is an odd provision in regard to indemnities in that there is no exclusion in respect of the employer's negligence. ASI MW is similar, shorter, and there is no provision for the employer to insure new work.

MW 80 contains very short insurance provisions. The level of risk to be insured is equivalent to 'specified perils' in JCT 80. The contractor is to insure new works and the employer is to insure existing works. In the latter case, there is no provision for determination of the contractor's employment if just and equitable after loss or damage to the property. Although either party may be required by the other as appropriate to show proof of insurance, neither has power to insure in case of default. There is no provision for insurance to be taken out against damage to other property not due to negligence and there is no provision for liquidated damages insurance. In other respects, the wording of the clause is similar to JCT 80.

The Fixed Fee form has insurance provisions similar to those contained in JCT 80 before Amendment 2 was issued. They are considered by many to be defective in the indemnity provisions in that any degree of contributory negligence on the part of the employer might be held to remove the contractor's indemnity obligation in its entirety. The level of risk to be insured is equivalent to 'specified perils' under JCT 80. The employer is responsible for insuring the works whether new or existing. The works are expressed to be at the 'sole risk' of the employer rather than in joint names. There is no provision for liquidated damages insurance.

ACA 2 insurance clauses are very straightforward in intention, and very broadly appear to provide for eventualities similar to JCT 80. The actual contingencies are to be spelled out in the policy. There is no provision for the employer to insure new works nor for liquidated damages insurance. There is, however, an optional clause which provides for the contractor to take out design indemnity insurance for the limit of indemnity stated in the contract documents. This is a major consideration if the contractor is to be responsible for any part of the design.

ASI has an indemnity clause against injury or damage to persons or property which is difficult to understand. The contractor is to indemnify unless the damage is due to negligence of the contractor or employer, in which case the

**6.6**   Insurance

negligent party will be liable. It appears that if the contractor is negligent, he will be liable, but he will be under no obligation to indemnify the employer. The remainder of the provisions approximately follow JCT 80 terms. However, from a strict interpretation of the wording, it appears that either party may determine the contractor's employment after loss or damage caused by insured risks, whether the work is to new or existing buildings. There is no liquidated damages insurance. Provisions are compared in Table 6.3.

**Table 6.3** Insurance provisions

| | JCT 80 With Quantities | JCT 80 With Approximate Quantities | JCT 80 Without Quantities | IFC 84 Intermediate Form | MW80 Minor Works Form | JCT 81 With Contractor's Design | JCT Fixed Fee Form | JCT 87 Management Contract | ACA 2 | ASI | ASI SW | ASI MW |
|---|---|---|---|---|---|---|---|---|---|---|---|---|
| Indemnity/insurance: injury to persons | • | • | • | • | • | • | • | • | • | • | • | • |
| Indemnity/insurance: damage to property | • | • | • | • | • | • | • | • | • | • | • | • |
| Employer's liability | • | • | • | • | – | • | • | • | • | • | • | • |
| Sub-/works-contractors included as insured | • | • | • | • | – | • | – | • | – | – | – | – |
| All risks | • | • | • | • | – | • | – | • | – | – | – | – |
| Specified perils or similar | • | • | • | • | • | • | • | • | • | • | • | • |
| New works insured by contractor | • | • | • | • | • | • | – | • | • | • | • | • |
| New works insured by employer | • | • | • | • | – | • | • | – | – | • | • | – |
| Alterations to existing insured by employer | • | • | • | • | • | • | • | • | • | • | • | • |
| Liquidated damages insurance | • | • | • | • | – | • | – | • | – | – | – | – |
| Design indemnity | – | – | – | – | – | – | – | – | • | – | – | – |

**6   Key provisions compared**

**6.7**
**Extension of time, damages**
**for delay**

The contractor's obligation to complete the works by the contract date for completion is removed if the employer interferes with or obstructs the works. If there is no fixed date for completion, the employer cannot deduct liquidated damages because there must be a definite date from which the damages can run. In such a situation the employer would be left to recover such damages as he could prove. It is principally for this reason that extension of time clauses are included in standard forms of contract; so as to preserve a completion date. They do of course serve the purpose of excusing the contractor from paying liquidated damages if an extension is given for a reason listed in the clause.

The architect may only give an extension of time for the reasons listed in the contract. It is, therefore, important that the reasons cover as many instances of employer obstruction or interference as possible if the employer's right to deduct liquidated damages is to be preserved.

There are 14 'relevant events' or reasons for which the architect can grant an extension of time under the provisions of JCT 80 With Quantities, JCT 80 Without Quantities and JCT 80 With Approximate Quantities. What can be termed employer's default are:

- Compliance with architect's instructions.
- Late information.
- Employer's men or materials.
- Failure to give access.
- Deferment of possession.

The extension of time clause provides for the contractor to notify all delays and give details, identify relevant events and give estimates in each case of the extent to which the contract completion date is likely to be exceeded.

The architect must grant a fair and reasonable extension of time no later than 12 weeks after receipt of reasonably sufficient particulars. If the contract completion date is less than 12 weeks away, the architect must give any extension before completion date. After contract completion date, if it occurs before, or no later than 12 weeks after, practical completion, the architect must carry out a review and either confirm the existing completion date, fix a later date or an earlier date if taking account of omissions warrants it.

JCT 81 provisions are very similar except that 'employer' is substituted for 'architect' and some of the relevant events are amended to take account of the contractor's design function and thus his reliance on statutory approvals. IFC 84 is broadly similar, but there are some significant differences. It is altogether less detailed and no time periods are inserted. The architect's duty is to estimate the extension of time 'so soon as he is able'. The events include the same employer's defaults as JCT 80, but the contractor's inability to obtain labour or materials is made optional. The architect is given express power to grant extension of time if the employer's default occurs after the contract completion date.

The Fixed Fee form bears a close family resemblance to JCT 63. Therefore, it has no time periods for the giving of extensions, there is no provision for a review after practical completion and extensions previously given cannot be reduced to take account of omissions from the work. The relevant events do not include failure to give access to the site or deferment of possession.

JCT 87 has extension of time provisions which are clearly cast in the same mould as JCT 80. The reasons for extension are termed 'project extension items' which are:

- Any cause which prevents the contractor properly carrying out his duties including employer's default, late information and deferment of possession.
- Any relevant event, other than delay by other works contractors, which entitles the works contractor to an extension of time.

The contractor must notify the architect if he intends to give an extension to a works contractor, but the architect has no power to do anything other than express dissent.

ACA 2 has optional provisions. Under one option, the contractor is entitled to extension of time only for reasons which may be broadly termed employer's default. The other option widens the grounds to include *force majeure*, damage due to insured risks, war, and so on, and delay caused by government agency, local authority or statutory undertaker. The contractor's duties are similar, but not the same as those under JCT 80. He is to notify delays which are likely to cause the taking over of the works on the due date to be prevented, including estimates of the extension. The architect must give the extension, if any, within 60 working days of receipt of all particulars and there is provision for a review. However, the architect may not reduce extensions already given.

ASI form provides for extensions in clause 4.4. The scheme is similar to JCT 80, but there are some differences: the contractor may not submit a notice or claim later than four weeks after practical completion. The contractor is also required to provide what is referred to as a 'reasoned case' to support his notice.

**Table 6.4**
Extension of time clauses

Column key:
- JCT 80 (all versions, clause 25.4)
- IFC 84 Intermediate Form (clause 2.3)
- MW 80 Minor Works Form (clause 2.2)
- JCT 81 With Contractor's Design (clause 25.4)
- JCT Fixed Fee Form (clause 19)
- JCT 87 Management Contract (clause 2.13)
- ACA 2 alternative 1 (clause 11.5)
- ACA 2 alt. 2 & BPF/ACA (clause 11.5)
- ASI (clause 4.45)
- ASI SW (clause 4.4)
- ASI MW (clause 4

| Grounds for extension | JCT 80 | IFC 84 | MW 80 | JCT 81 | JCT Fixed Fee | JCT 87 | ACA 2 alt 1 | ACA 2 alt 2 & BPF/ACA | ASI | ASI SW | ASI MW |
|---|---|---|---|---|---|---|---|---|---|---|---|
| Force majeure | • | • | – | • | • | • | – | • | • | – | – |
| Exceptionally adverse weather conditions | • | • | – | • | – | • | – | – | • | – | – |
| Exceptionally inclement weather | – | – | – | – | • | – | – | – | – | – | – |
| Damage due to insured risks | • | • | – | • | – | • | – | • | • | – | – |
| Civil commotion, riot, rebellion | • | • | – | • | • | • | – | • | • | – | – |
| Strikes and lock-outs | • | • | – | • | • | • | – | – | • | – | – |
| War, hostilities, invasion | • | • | – | • | • | • | – | • | – | – | – |
| Compliance with specified architect's instructions | • | • | • | • | • | • | – | – | • | – | – |
| Late instructions, etc. | • | • | – | • | • | • | – | • | • | – | – |
| Delay on the part of nominated sub-contractors or suppliers | • | – | – | – | • | • | – | – | • | – | – |
| Employer's direct work or supply of materials | • | • | – | • | • | • | – | – | • | – | – |
| Exercise of governmental power | • | – | – | • | – | • | – | – | • | – | – |
| Contractor's unforeseeable inability to obtain labour or materials | • | • | – | • | • | • | – | – | • | – | – |
| Work under statutory powers by statutory undertakers | • | • | – | • | • | • | – | • | • | – | – |
| Employer's failure to give access | • | • | – | • | – | • | – | – | • | – | – |
| Deferment of possession | • | • | – | • | – | • | – | – | – | – | – |
| Default of employer | – | – | – | – | • | • | • | – | – | – | – |
| Any other reason beyond control of contractor: Foreseen | – | – | • | – | – | – | – | – | – | – | – |
| Unforeseen | – | – | • | – | – | – | – | – | • | – | – |
| Delay in receipt of necessary permission of statutory body | – | – | – | • | – | – | – | – | – | – | – |
| Antiquities | – | – | – | – | – | – | – | – | • | – | – |
| Approximate quantities not reasonably accurate | • | • | – | – | – | – | – | – | – | – | – |
| If warranted | – | – | – | – | – | – | – | – | – | • | • |

## 6.7 Extension of time, damages for delay

Not later than four weeks after practical completion, he must supply the architect with a summary case for the total extension of time he wishes to claim. There is express provision for the architect to consider any request or claim in connection with a variation ordered after practical completion of the works.

The causes of delay are similar to JCT 80 provisions, but there is no provision for deferment of possession and, therefore, no provision for an extension of time under that head. There is a strange provision relating to 'significant delays or frustration caused by the Employer over access...' the meaning of which is obscure.

MW 80 extension provisions are very simple. The grounds for extension are wider than most since the contractor is entitled to an extension for delay due to reasons beyond his control, including architect's instructions which are not a result of the contractor's default. It appears, for example, that adverse weather conditions would qualify even if not exceptionally adverse. Whether the clause is sufficiently precise to allow extension of time for all employer's default has been the subject of debate. Some commentators think not and the introduction of the reference to architect's instructions appears to support the argument for a restricted interpretation of the clause. The contractor is obliged to notify only of those delays which clearly will prevent completion by the due date. ASI SW provides for the contractor to give prompt notice of delay, giving reasons and estimate of delay beyond completion date. The architect is given 'absolute discretion' to grant any extension of time 'warranted'. ASI MW has very similar, but even shorter, provisions and it must be doubtful whether either form effectively safeguards the employer if he is responsible for any part of a delay.

All forms of contract make provision for the employer to deduct liquidated damages if the contractor fails to complete the works by the completion date or any extended date. In general, all forms have the same preconditions as part of their terms: a notice of non-completion must be given if the contractor fails to complete by the due date. If the employer wishes to deduct liquidated damages, he must first serve notice of his intention on the contractor. There are exceptions to this general procedure which should be noted.

No certificate or notices whatsoever are required under MW 80. Under the terms of the Fixed Fee form, the architect seems to have the option of not issuing a certificate of non-completion, but the employer does not need to notify the contractor before deducting liquidated damages. The ACA 2 form gives the option of unliquidated damages. In that case the architect must issue his non-completion certificate and the employer may then deduct such damage, loss and/or expense as he has suffered as a result of the delayed taking over. Where unliquidated damages are specified, the architect's certificate is required, but nothing else. The employer may not deduct, but he may require the architect to deduct the damages from amounts otherwise payable on any certificate. The ASI form of contract requires no certificates before deduction of liquidated damages, but the architect is required to assess and confirm the period of delay to the employer and the contractor. In the case of ASI SW, the contractor is to pay liquidated damages for the period of delay certified by the architect. Under ASI MW terms, the wording is uncertain in meaning and although the adviser is to certify delay for the purpose of payment of liquidated damages, the precise circumstances which will lead the contractor to pay damages are not set out. It seems unlikely that the liquidated damages provision could be enforced under this form.

All forms of contract, with the exception of ACA 2, require the contractor to complete 'on or before' the date for completion. The contractor may therefore finish before the due date. ACA 2, which requires the contractor to have the works ready for taking-over on the date for taking over in the time schedule, appears to restrict the contractor to completion on the due date. Grounds for extension of time are compared in Table 6.4.

## 6.8 Assignment and sub-letting

Under the general law, either party to a contract may assign his rights, but neither party may assign his obligations without the other's consent. All the standard forms forbid assignment of the contract without consent. ACA 2 then very sensibly proceeds to allow the contractor to assign his right to receive payment (without such right many contractors would be unable to raise the initial capital required to start the project) and the employer may assign his rights under the contract after taking over of the works. This recognises the fact that many buildings are developed for the express purpose of selling on or leasing as soon as, or even before, they are completed. JCT 80 in all its versions, JCT 81 and JCT 87 contain a clause which, if the employer has stated that it is to apply, enables the employer to assign to any future lessee or purchaser the right to bring proceedings against the contractor.

All the forms allow sub-letting with the architect's consent. In the case of JCT 81, it is the employer's consent which is required and there is an additional provision for the contractor to sub-let design. ASI requires the contractor to supply the architect with a list of proposed sub-contractors. It is likely that one of the reasons for the architect reasonably refusing consent under the other standard forms would be if the contractor refused to reveal the name of a proposed sub-contractor or if the architect had bad experiences of a particular sub-contractor.

All the JCT 80 versions provide for the employer to include work to be carried out by a sub-contractor chosen by the contractor from a list of at least three. This is a very useful alternative to nomination which is also provided for in JCT 80. The provisions are thorough, but extremely complex and difficult to apply correctly. A considerable amount of sub-contract documentation is produced for tendering, nomination, warranty and sub-contract purposes, the procedures for which must be well advanced before main contract tendering takes place if the nomination is to proceed smoothly. Nomination is also referred to in the Fixed Fee form on terms which are very similar to JCT 63 terms. It follows, therefore, that they are far less comprehensive than the JCT 80 terms. Decided cases may fill some of the gaps.

ASI merely provides for the architect to nominate specialist firms to carry out work. The provisions are very brief and make no reference to renomination on failure of the nominated sub-contractor. ASI SW has similar, but briefer, provisions. Neither of these two forms can be considered to make satisfactory provision for nomination. IFC 84 has provision for naming persons as sub-contractors. Although heralded as far simpler than JCT nomination provisions, they are in fact quite complex although shorter than JCT 80 nomination terms. There is considerable supporting documentation. ACA 2 has provisions for the naming of sub-contractors. Apart from two instances of ambiguity, the terms have much to recommend them. They are short, they are comprehensive, the onus for design and other sub-contract defects is firmly on the shoulders of the contractor who may also deal with the situation if the original named sub-contractor fails.

If the optional supplementary provisions are stated to apply, JCT 81 has provision for naming persons as sub-contractors. They appear to owe something to both the IFC 84 and the ACA 2 provisions, but it must be questioned whether the use of this provision in the context of a design and construct contract is sensible.

**6  Key provisions compared**

JCT 87 has no provisions for nomination or naming. The nearest equivalent is the works contractor provisions which form an essential part of the whole philosophy of this form. A comparison of the provisions is to be found in Table 6.5.

**Table 6.5**
Assignment and sub-letting

| | JCT 80 With Quantities | JCT 80 With Approximate Quantities | JCT 80 Without Quantities | IFC 84 Intermediate Form | MW80 Minor Works Form | JCT 81 With Contractor's Design | JCT Fixed Fee Form | JCT 87 Management Contract | ACA 2 | ASI | ASI SW | ASI MW |
|---|---|---|---|---|---|---|---|---|---|---|---|---|
| No assignment without consent | ● | ● | ● | ● | ● | ● | ● | – | – | ● | ● | ● |
| No assignment of duties without consent | – | – | – | – | – | – | – | – | ● | – | – | – |
| No sub-letting without consent | ● | ● | ● | ● | ● | ● | ● | – | ● | ● | ● | ● |
| Choice from list of three | ● | ● | ● | – | – | – | – | – | – | – | – | – |
| Nomination provision | ● | ● | ● | – | – | – | ● | – | – | ● | ● | – |
| Renomination provision | ● | ● | ● | – | – | – | – | – | – | – | – | – |
| Named person provision | – | – | – | ● | – | – | – | – | – | – | – | – |
| Named sub-contractors | – | – | – | – | – | – | – | ● | – | – | – | – |
| Direct payment possible | ● | ● | ● | – | – | – | ● | – | – | ● | ● | – |

**6.9 Payment**

JCT 80 in all versions has very complex and detailed provisions for payment. IFC 84 has less complex provisions, but the general scheme is much the same. Payments are to be made on certificates issued by the architect at regular intervals as stated in the Appendix, after a valuation if required. There are detailed provisions regarding the amounts to be included. Retention may be deducted and there is a strict timetable for the issue of a final certificate which is stated to be conclusive on certain matters. The Fixed Fee form follows a similar scheme, but the final certificate is conclusive only on the matters of the architect's satisfaction, where materials and workmanship have been so specified and the clauses regulating payment have been properly applied. ASI form owes much to JCT 80, but there is provision for the contractor to make application for payment if there is no quantity surveyor. The final certificate is not conclusive. ASI SW is much the same. The quantity surveyor's involvement depends on the use of the Supplementary Conditions. Under JCT 87 provisions the architect is to certify an appropriate proportion of the management fee in each certificate together with the prime cost of the work. In this there are similarities to the situation under the Fixed Fee form. The final certificate is conclusive to the same extent as under JCT 80. Under JCT 81, there is no architect and the employer is to pay the interim amounts properly due. Payment may be made either following a system of interim payments somewhat similar to JCT 80, or in stage payments, the stages to be agreed by the parties and entered into the appendix before the contract is executed. The final certificate is conclusive to the same extent as JCT 80.

ACA 2 payment terms are very simple. The onus is on the contractor to submit monthly applications. There is a strict timetable for the issue of the final certificate which is not expressed as conclusive in any respect. MW 80 provides that the contractor's request triggers the architect's certification of progress payments. As might be expected, the provisions are brief, but adequate for the type of work envisaged. ASI MW has a simple payment scheme under which payment may be in the form of one sum, payable after the contractor's final account is approved and the adviser has issued his final certificate. An option is for the adviser to certify payments to the contractor from time to time at the adviser's discretion. The final certificate is not conclusive in regard to any matter.

Fluctuations fall into one of three categories:

a) Contribution, levy and tax.

b) Labour and materials cost.

c) Price adjustment formula.

JCT 80 With Quantities, JCT 80 Without quantities, JCT 81 and ASI forms allow for all three types. JCT 80 With Approximate Quantities limits fluctuations to (b) and (c), IFC 84 includes only (a) and (c), ASI SW includes only (a) and (b), and MW 80 and ASI MW have provision for only (a). The Fixed Fee form and JCT 87 have no provision for fluctuation because the prime cost is payable and, in the case of JCT 87, fluctuations are dealt with in the works contracts. ACA 2 deals with fluctuations by means of its own formula system of ACA indices. Payments provisions are compared in Table 6.6.

**6**   Key provisions compared

**Table 6.6**
Payment

| | JCT 80 With Quantities | JCT 80 With Approximate Quantities | JCT 80 Without Quantities | IFC 84 Intermediate Form | MW80 Minor Works Form | JCT 81 With Contractor's Design | JCT Fixed Fee Form | JCT 87 Management Contract | ACA 2 | ASI | ASI SW | ASI MW |
|---|---|---|---|---|---|---|---|---|---|---|---|---|
| Architect's certificates | ● | ● | ● | ● | ● | – | ● | ● | ● | ● | ● | ● |
| Regular interim | ● | ● | ● | ● | ● | ● | ● | ● | ● | ● | ● | ● |
| Stage | – | – | – | ● | – | ● | – | – | – | – | – | ● |
| Prior QS valuation | ● | ● | ● | ● | – | – | – | ● | ● | ● | ● | – |
| Contractor to apply | – | – | – | – | – | ● | – | – | ● | ● | ● | – |
| Possible payment for off-site goods | ● | ● | ● | ● | – | ● | ● | – | ● | – | – | – |
| Retention | ● | ● | ● | ● | ● | ● | ● | ● | ● | ● | ● | ● |
| Balance released at M/G of defects | ● | ● | ● | – | – | ● | ● | ● | – | – | – | – |
| Balance released at final certificate | – | – | – | ● | ● | – | – | – | ● | ● | ● | ● |
| Final certificate/account conclusive: | | | | | | | | | | | | |
| amount | ● | ● | ● | ● | – | ● | ● | ● | – | – | – | – |
| satisfaction | ● | ● | ● | ● | – | ● | ● | ● | – | – | – | – |
| extensions | ● | ● | ● | ● | – | ● | – | ● | – | – | – | – |
| loss and/or expense | ● | ● | ● | ● | – | ● | – | ● | – | – | – | – |
| Fluctuations: | | | | | | | | | | | | |
| contribution, levy, tax | ● | – | ● | – | ● | ● | – | – | – | ● | ● | ● |
| labour and materials | ● | ● | ● | – | – | ● | – | – | – | ● | ● | – |
| formula | ● | ● | ● | – | – | ● | – | – | ● | ● | – | – |

## 6.10 Loss and/or expense

Every standard form has some provision for the contractor to recover direct loss and/or expense caused by specified matters affecting the regular progress of the works. In each case, except MW 80, the contractor must make application as soon as it is reasonably apparent that regular progress is being or is likely to be disrupted. Application may be made only in respect of the matters listed. The contractor need not recover under the contractual machinery. He may, in respect of those matters which are breaches of contract, sue for damages at common law.

There are considerable advantages in attempting to recover through the contract because not all the matters listed in the loss and/or expense clauses are breaches. JCT 80 in all versions include:

- Late information.
- Opening up and testing.
- Discrepancies between documents.
- Employer's men or materials.
- Postponement.
- Failure to give access.
- Compliance with architect's instructions.
- Approximate quantities not a reasonably accurate forecast.
- Deferment of possession.

JCT 81 is almost identical, but with the addition of delay in obtaining development control permission. There is an alternative system under the optional provisions which is very like the provisions in ACA 2. IFC 84 is a simpler version of the JCT 80 provisions, but including a similar list of matters. The Fixed Fee form provisions do not include deferment or failure on the part of the employer to give access. They are otherwise similar to JCT 63 provisions.

The ASI provisions do not include deferment, but they do include 'frustration by the employer over access to the site'. The meaning of this phrase is uncertain since 'frustration' has a precise legal meaning which does not permit it to be used in this way. Taking 'frustration' in its ordinary everyday meaning does not assist in revealing the sense. One is left to little better than guess-work regarding the true intent of this particular clause. This form also requires the submission of a reasoned case in support of the claim. If more than one claim is made, a summary claim must be submitted no later than four weeks after practical completion.

The ACA 2 terms provide for the architect to be able to consider all claims based on the actions or defaults of the employer – effectively, all common law claims against the employer arising out of the contract. It is possible that the wording of the clause allows the contractor to claim consequential losses also. The system envisages that the contractor will make monthly applications with estimates so long as the loss and/or expense continues. The architect must take speedy action to deal with the applications as they arrive. The system has the advantage of simplicity.

MW 80 has provision for the architect to include for loss and/or expense caused by compliance with his instructions, but if the contractor wishes to claim for any other reason, he must take action at common law. JCT 87 has no provision for financial claims from the contractor. It is expected that he will simply refer claims from individual works contractors.

**Table 6.7**
Loss and/or expense

| Grounds | JCT 80 With Quantities | JCT 80 With Approximate Quantities | JCT 80 Without Quantities | IFC 84 Intermediate Form | MW80 Minor Works Form | JCT 81 With Contractor's Design | JCT Fixed Fee Form | JCT 87 Management Contract | ACA 2 | ASI | ASI SW | ASI MW |
|---|---|---|---|---|---|---|---|---|---|---|---|---|
| Late information | ● | ● | ● | ● | – | ● | ● | – | – | ● | – | – |
| Opening up and testing | ● | ● | ● | ● | – | ● | ● | – | – | ● | – | – |
| Discrepancies | ● | ● | ● | ● | – | – | – | – | – | ● | – | – |
| Employer's men | ● | ● | ● | ● | – | ● | ● | – | – | ● | – | – |
| Employer's materials | ● | ● | ● | ● | – | ● | – | – | – | ● | – | – |
| Postponement of work | ● | ● | ● | ● | – | ● | ● | – | – | ● | – | – |
| Employer's failure to give access | ● | ● | ● | ● | – | ● | – | – | – | ● | – | – |
| Variations and provisional sums | ● | ● | ● | ● | ● | ● | – | – | – | ● | – | – |
| Deferment of possession | ● | ● | ● | ● | – | ● | – | – | – | – | – | – |
| Instructions regarding order of work | ● | ● | ● | ● | ● | ● | ● | – | – | – | – | – |
| Delay in development control permission | – | – | – | – | – | ● | – | – | – | – | – | – |
| Approximate quantities not reasonably accurate | ● | ● | ● | ● | – | – | – | – | – | – | – | – |
| Act, omission, default or negligence of employer or architect | – | – | – | – | – | – | – | – | ● | – | – | – |
| Arising under the contract | – | – | – | – | – | – | – | – | – | – | ● | – |

Under ASI SW provisions, there is no list of matters which entitle the contractor to make application for loss and/or expense. The contractor must make any claims not later than four weeks from practical completion and the architect is given the power to consider the claim and certify any amount warranted. If this clause is effective, it gives the architect power to consider what would be common law claims under other

**6.10** Loss and/or expense

contracts. It is likely that the architect would not be able to consider claims for such things as disruption due to opening up and testing. There is no breach of contract involved because the architect is expressly empowered to issue such an instruction. There is no effective clause to enable the contractor to recover loss and/or expense under ASI MW. Table 6.7 compares provisions.

**6.11**
**Termination**

JCT 80 in all versions provides for determination of the contractor's employment by employer or contractor if the other makes default in respect of one of the areas listed. From the employer's point of view, the most important reasons are the contractor's suspension of the works, failure to work regularly and diligently, failure to comply with notice to remove defective work if the works are substantially affected as a result, and the contractor's insolvency.

The most important reasons why the contractor may determine are the employer's failure to pay, interference with certificates, suspension of the works as a result of any of a list of actions on the part of the employer or insolvency. It should be noted that, although the employer must serve notice of default before determination (except in the case of insolvency), the contractor is required to serve prior notice only if the employer fails to pay. There are extensive provisions to govern the conduct of the parties after determination. The principal difference is that if the employer determines, he may employ and pay others to finish the work and he need not pay anything further to the original contractor until the project is complete. At that stage, the employer may charge all his loss and/or damage caused by the determination. If the contractor determines, he must be paid for everything he has done immediately together with loss and/or damage caused by the determination.

There is also special provision for determination by either party if the works are suspended for stipulated periods as a result of specified matters which are the fault of neither party. The consequences are as if the contractor had determined except that he is not entitled to loss and/or damage. Provision is also made for determination as a result of war or damage caused by insurance risks in the case of existing buildings.

IFC 84 is in very similar terms. An important difference, however, is that the contractor is required to give prior notice in every instance, except insolvency, before determining. JCT 81 is virtually identical except that the employer may determine if the contractor suspends the design work without reasonable cause and the contractor may determine if delay in receipt of development control permission causes suspension of the works for a stipulated period. As part of the consequences, whoever determines, the contractor must supply the employer with two copies of all drawings.

The Fixed Fee form is similar in its terms to JCT 80, but the 'neutral' events are included in grounds for contractor determination with the result that suspension of the works due to insured risks for a continuous period named in the Appendix could enable the contractor to determine and collect, among other things, the loss of profit he would have made if the project had continued. This is a significant disadvantage for the employer which was present in JCT 63 and JCT 80 until Amendment 4.

JCT 87 is similar to JCT 80, but there is an additional clause which allows the employer to determine the contractor's employment at will. The consequences are designed to protect the contractor's interests.

ACA 2 follows in much the same as JCT 80 terms, but there is no automatic entitlement to loss and/or damage under the terms of the contract. If either party considers that they are so entitled an action must be founded at common law. Either party may refer the dispute to the adjudicator within 20 days of termination otherwise a party's entitlement to terminate cannot be challenged.

ASI form owes much to JCT 80. Significant differences include the employer's duty to give two notices before determination and the contractor's right to determine if the employer or reasons beyond the contractor's control delay the work for four continous weeks. There is a clear provision that the contractor must give up possession of the site whichever party determines. ASI SW has shorter terms to much the same effect. The employer is not required to give notice before determination. ASI MW is similar, but the consequences are restricted in comparison.

MW 80 is brief. The employer need not give prior notice. There are only three grounds: suspension of work, failure to proceed regularly and diligently, and insolvency. The contractor must give prior notice for lack of payment, interference with a certificate or suspension of the work for a month, but no notice is needed in the case of the employer's insolvency. The provisions governing the conduct of the parties after determination are not comprehensive and it may be that, if either party can bring the contract to an end under the general law, the common law remedies may be better than the contractual ones. See Table 6.8 for a comparison of termination grounds.

**6.11**  Termination

**Table 6.8**
Termination clauses

| Clause | JCT 80 (all versions) | IFC 84 Intermediate Form | MW 80 Minor Works Form | JCT 81 With Contractor's Design | JCT Fixed Fee Form | JCT 87 Management Contract | ACA 2 | ASI | ASI SW | ASI MW |
|---|---|---|---|---|---|---|---|---|---|---|
| **By employer** | | | | | | | | | | |
| Contractor wholly suspends work | • | • | • | • | • | • | • | • | • | • |
| Contractor fails to proceed regularly and diligently with the works | • | • | • | • | • | • | • | • | • | • |
| Contractor does not comply with instruction re defective work | • | • | – | • | • | • | • | • | • | • |
| Contractor assigns without consent | • | • | – | • | • | • | • | – | – | – |
| Contractor becomes insolvent | • | • | • | • | • | • | • | • | • | • |
| Contractor corrupt | • | • | • | • | – | • | – | • | – | – |
| Contractor otherwise in breach of contract | – | – | – | – | – | – | – | – | – | – |
| At the employer's discretion | – | – | – | – | • | – | • | – | – | – |
| **By contractor** | | | | | | | | | | |
| Non-payment | • | • | • | • | • | • | • | • | • | • |
| Obstruction by employer | • | • | • | – | • | • | • | • | – | – |
| Four weeks continuous delay by employer | – | – | – | – | – | – | – | • | • | • |
| Persistent interruption of progress | – | – | – | – | – | – | – | • | – | – |
| Delay in works for specified period due to: | | | | | | | | | | |
| *Force majeure* | – | – | – | – | • | – | – | – | – | – |
| Damage by insurance contingencies | – | – | – | – | • | – | – | • | – | – |
| Civil commotion | – | – | – | – | • | – | – | – | – | – |
| Certain AIs | • | • | – | • | • | • | – | – | – | – |
| Late instructions | • | • | – | • | • | • | – | – | – | – |
| Delay by employer's men | • | • | – | • | • | • | – | – | – | – |
| Reasons beyond contractor's control | – | – | – | – | – | – | – | • | – | – |
| Opening up and testing | • | – | – | • | • | • | – | – | – | – |
| Planning approval | – | – | – | • | – | – | – | – | – | – |
| Failure to give access | – | • | – | – | • | – | – | – | – | – |
| Employer's breach | – | – | • | – | – | – | – | – | – | – |
| Employer becomes insolvent, etc. | • | • | • | – | • | – | • | • | • | • |
| **By either party** | | | | | | | | | | |
| Damage to existing works due to insurance contingencies | • | • | – | • | • | – | – | – | – | – |
| Outbreak of hostilities | • | – | – | • | • | – | – | – | – | – |
| Suspension of work for a specified period due to: | | | | | | | | | | |
| *Force majeure* | • | • | – | – | – | • | • | – | – | – |
| Damage by insurance contingencies | • | • | – | – | – | • | • | – | – | – |
| Civil commotion | • | • | – | – | – | • | – | – | – | – |
| War etc. | – | – | – | – | – | – | • | – | – | – |

**6.12**
**Disputes**

All the standard forms provide for disputes to be settled by arbitration. It is now settled that an arbitrator under most standard forms has wider powers to open up and review decisions and certificates than would a judge if the matter came before a court. The ACA 2 form, however, has provision for the parties to decide on one of three options: adjudication plus arbitration, arbitration, or litigation. The adjudication option appears to have much to offer. JCT 80 in all versions, IFC 84 and JCT 87 contain sophisticated arbitration provisions which provide for the parties to agree on an arbitrator or, failing agreement, for either party to request the appointment by a designated third party. The arbitrator is given his usual wide powers including rectification and the arbitration is to be conducted under JCT Arbitration Rules which provide for a strict timescale and the type of hearing to suit circumstances. A useful provision allows the joining of arbitrations on related matters.

JCT 81 is almost identical, but there is no provision for the joining of related matters. By the optional supplementary provisions, adjudication can be invoked during the course of the work in respect of certain matters. This is clearly a very useful term.

MW 80 is similar to JCT 80 terms, but very much shorter and the JCT Arbitration Rules are made optional. As might be expected, there is no provision for joining sub-contract disputes. The Fixed Fee form provisions follow the old JCT 63 lines. There is no joining procedure. The ASI form has a procedure which seems to owe something to the ICE form in that disputes must first be referred to the architect. What follows is unclear. There is provision for joining related arbitrations and for a shortened procedure.

Under both ASI SW and ASI MW the procedure is arbitration, but the arbitrator is given no special powers. A dispute is first to be put to the architect (or adviser under ASI MW) for a decision, but there is no time limit imposed. Clauses are compared in Table 6.9.

**6.12**    Disputes

**Table 6.9**

Disputes

| | JCT 80 With Quantities | JCT 80 With Approximate Quantities | JCT 80 Without Quantities | IFC 84 Intermediate Form | MW80 Minor Works Form | JCT 81 With Contractor's Design | JCT Fixed Fee Form | JCT 87 Management Contract | ACA 2 | ASI | ASI SW | ASI MW |
|---|---|---|---|---|---|---|---|---|---|---|---|---|
| 'Joining' provisions | ● | ● | ● | ● | – | – | – | ● | ● | ● | – | – |
| Arbitration restricted before completion | ● | ● | ● | – | – | ● | ● | ● | – | ● | – | – |
| Arbitration not restricted before completion | – | – | – | ● | ● | – | – | – | – | – | ● | ● |
| No arbitration before completion | – | – | – | – | – | – | – | ● | – | – | – | – |
| Arbitrator expressly given wide powers | ● | ● | ● | ● | ● | ● | ● | ● | ● | ● | – | – |
| Express power to rectify contract | ● | ● | ● | ● | ● | ● | – | ● | – | – | – | – |
| Agreement for appeals etc. | ● | ● | ● | ● | – | ● | – | ● | – | – | – | – |
| Substitute arbitrator | ● | ● | ● | ● | ● | ● | – | ● | – | – | – | – |
| Adjudication option | – | – | – | – | – | ● | – | – | ● | – | – | – |
| Architect's decision as first stage | – | – | – | – | – | – | – | – | ● | ● | ● | ● |
| JCT Arbitration Rules: mandatory | ● | ● | ● | ● | – | ● | – | ● | – | – | – | – |
| optional | – | – | – | – | ● | – | – | – | – | – | – | – |

# 7 Choice of contract

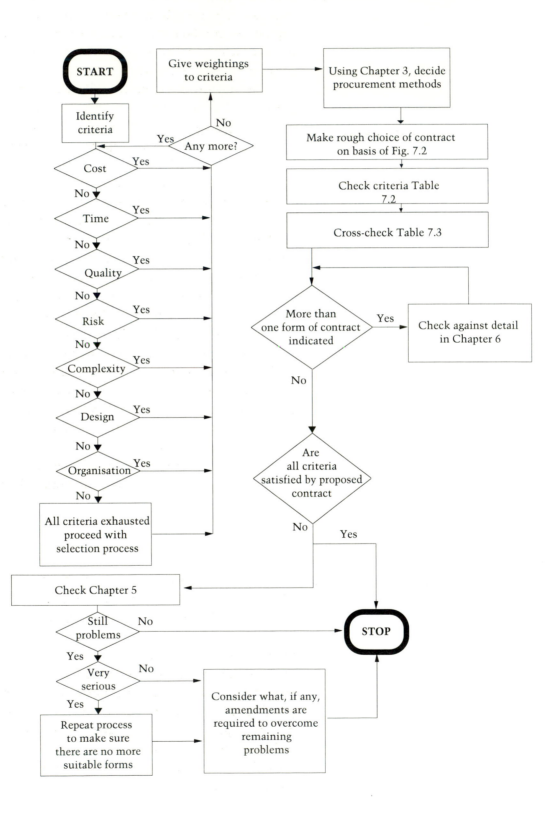

**Fig. 7.1** Methodology of choice.

**7.1 Introduction**

The purpose of this chapter is to suggest a methodology for choosing the most suitable form of contract for a given situation. The criteria discussed in Chapter 2 will indicate the appropriate method of building procurement, and the criteria together with the chosen procurement method should lead to the correct form of contract.

The appropriate contract will perfectly fit all criteria presented. Using a standard form of contract is rather like buying a standard motor car or a standard house. There is a variation between models, but the choice to be made is very basic. Once the choice is made, the particular model must be accepted complete with its disadvantages. The reason for choice is that the advantages of that particular model appear to outweigh the disadvantages. To take the analogy one stage further, a standard car can be 'customised' to fit more closely a customer's requirements just as a contract can be amended for the same purpose. A car can be created especially for a customer. A contract can be especially drafted for a client. Apart from anything else, large amendments or drafting of a contract is expensive and uncertain in its results.

It is therefore unlikely that any standard form will be perfectly suited to your client's needs. Your aim should be to advise the use of a form which has no obvious dangers. You should also be able to advise if there are any minor amendments which should be carried out (see section 7.5).

Aids such as flowcharts and choice tables help in choosing a suitable form, but once the 'rough' choice is made, fine tuning can only be achieved by studying the individual contract.

**7.2 Methodology**

1. Identify the selection criteria from Chapter 2.
2. With your client, decide priorities at this stage and give them weightings, that is: first priority – 12, second priority – 11 and so on.
3. On the basis of Chapter 3 and Table 7.1 decide on the possible procurement methods. There are likely to be several which will appear unsuitable. The first priority will eliminate many of the possible choices. When the second priority is added, a rethink may be required. The procurement path selected will largely influence the choice of contract.
4. With the information from 3, make a rough choice of contract using Fig. 7.2.

**Table 7.1**
Criteria and procurement methods

| Procurement criteria | Traditional • Competitive | Traditional • Negotiated/two-stage | Project management • Competitive | Project management • Negotiated/two-stage | Design and manage | Design and build | Management contracting | Construction management |
|---|---|---|---|---|---|---|---|---|
| Most appropriate = 1 | | | | | | | | |
| Least appropriate = 3 | | | | | | | | |
| Time • Economy | 2 | 3 | 2 | 3 | 2 | 1 | 1 | 2 |
| Time • Certainty | 1 | 2 | 1 | 2 | 2 | 1 | 1 | 2 |
| Cost • Economy | 1 | 3 | 1 | 3 | 2 | 3 | 3 | 3 |
| Cost • Certainty | 1 | 1 | 1 | 1 | 2 | 1 | 3 | 3 |
| Control • Risk to employer | 2 | 2 | 2 | 2 | 3 | 3 | 1 | 1 |
| Control • Risk to contractor | 2 | 2 | 2 | 2 | 1 | 1 | 3 | 3 |
| Quality• Design | 1 | 1 | 1 | 1 | 1 | 2 | 2 | 2 |
| Quality • Construction | 2 | 1 | 2 | 1 | 2 | 2 | 1 | 1 |
| Size/value • Medium–large | 1 | 1 | 1 | 1 | 1 | 1 | 1 | 1 |
| Size/value • Small–medium | 1 | 2 | 3 | 3 | 2 | 2 | 3 | 3 |
| Complexity • Complex | 1 | 1 | 1 | 1 | 3 | 3 | 1 | 1 |
| Complexity • Simple | 1 | 2 | 3 | 3 | 1 | 1 | 3 | 3 |

5. Confirm the choice by reference to the criteria Table 7.2.

6. Cross check the method of procurement to the form of contract Table 7.3.

7. It is conceivable that, at this stage, there are two possible forms of contract, but the selection process is more likely to have narrowed the choice to a single standard form.

8. The key provisions should be checked with the information in Chapter 6 using the tables as a first step and looking at the text for greater detail. This process should narrow the choice to one form.

9. Most of the criteria should be satisfied by this stage, but the next step is to isolate those aspects of the chosen form which appear not to satisfy criteria.

10. Check with the quick reference in Chapter 5. There may be no problems. If not, check the aspects in the standard form itself.

11. If problems still remain, consider whether the deficiencies are so serious as to pose an unacceptable risk to the employer or to

7   Choice of contract

make the form unsuitable. If so, you must eliminate the form and either repeat the process to choose another form or, if this is the most suitable form, consider amendment to remove the problems. If amendment is proposed, get expert help. Usually, there will be no necessity to carry out more than very basic amendments; they do, however, need care.

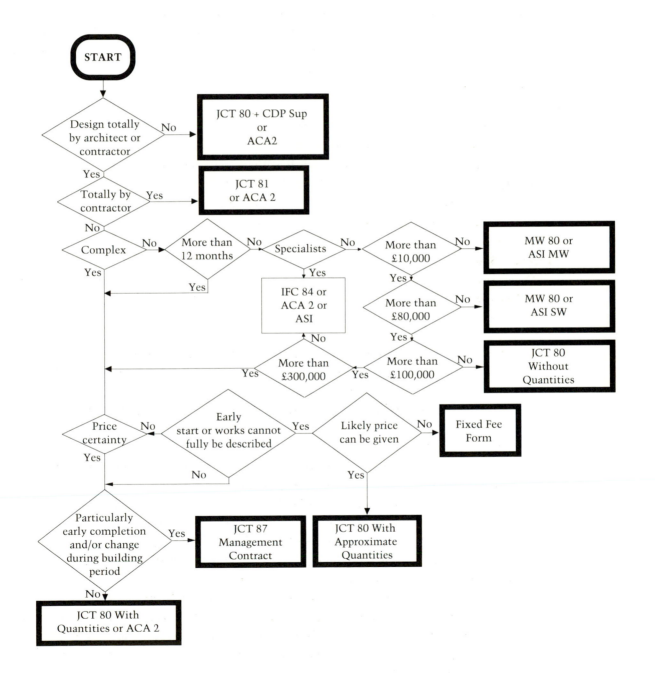

**Fig. 7.2** Contract choice.

**7.3**
**Worked examples**

Using words to describe an activity is a very inadequate system of explanation. Once you have worked through the method outlined above the rationale should become clear. Choosing a form using the system in this book may not be easy, but it is far easier than learning the contents of the standard forms. You do not have to follow the method outlined. You may opt for a more direct system of choice, but the tables, flowcharts and quick references contained in this book should assist you. If you do opt for this book's methodology, the following worked examples illustrate the system. Only the first of the examples has been worked out in the kind of detail required for contract selection.

**Table 7.2**
**Criteria**

| Criteria | JCT 80 With Quantities | JCT 80 With Approximate Quantities | JCT 80 Without Quantities | IFC 84 Intermediate Form | MW80 Minor Works Form | JCT 81 With Contractor's Design | JCT Fixed Fee Form | JCT 87 Management Contract | ACA 2 | ASI | ASI SW | ASI MW |
|---|---|---|---|---|---|---|---|---|---|---|---|---|
| Simple | - | - | - | - | ● | - | - | - | - | - | ● | ● |
| Comprehensive | ● | ● | ● | - | - | ● | - | ● | ● | - | - | - |
| Flexible | - | - | - | ● | - | ● | - | ● | ● | - | - | - |
| Negotiated | ● | ● | ● | ● | ● | ● | ● | ● | - | - | - | - |
| Bills of quantities | ● | ● | - | ● | - | - | - | - | ● | ● | ● | - |
| Specification | - | - | ● | ● | ● | - | ● | ● | ● | ● | ● | ● |
| Schedule of rates | - | - | - | ● | ● | - | - | - | ● | - | - | - |
| Complex work | ● | ● | - | - | - | - | - | ● | ● | - | - | - |
| Uncertain work | - | ● | - | - | - | - | ● | - | - | - | - | - |
| Early start | - | ● | - | - | - | - | ● | ● | - | - | - | - |
| Early finish | - | - | - | - | - | ● | - | ● | ● | - | - | - |
| Project management | - | - | - | - | - | - | ● | ● | ● | - | - | - |
| Contractor management | - | - | - | - | - | - | - | ● | - | - | - | - |
| Up to £10,000 | - | - | - | - | - | - | - | - | - | - | - | ● |
| Up to £80,000 | - | - | - | - | ● | - | - | - | - | - | ● | - |
| Up to £130,000 | - | - | ● | - | - | - | - | - | - | - | - | - |
| Up to £300,000 | ● | ● | - | ● | - | - | - | ● | - | ● | - | - |
| Over £300,000 | ● | ● | - | - | - | ● | - | ● | ● | - | - | - |
| Lump sum | ● | ● | ● | ● | ● | ● | - | - | ● | ● | ● | ● |
| Prime cost | - | - | - | - | - | - | ● | ● | - | - | - | - |
| Specialists can be used | ● | ● | ● | ● | - | - | ● | ● | ● | ● | ● | - |

### 7.3.1 Example

A national chain of supermarkets wishes to open a new store in a provincial town. The architect has extracted the following key elements from the employer's brief:

- The store must be opened as quickly as possible, but it is even more important that the opening date is fixed. Before that date, to enable certain specialised direct works to be carried out, portions of the building are required to be made available for the employer by key dates.

- The cost of the store is relatively unimportant, but the need to have the board of directors approve a budget means that the price should be fixed.

- It is essential that the design of the store, while making appropriate reference to the 'house style', incorporates the latest design thinking. The image is important. Independent architectural advice is required.

- The project will be relatively large, in the region of £6 to £8 million.

- Approximately 30% of the work will be carried out by specialist sub-contractors.

Giving approximate weightings might produce the result shown in Fig. 7.3. It will be noticed that a number of criteria have similar weightings. The next stage is to determine the most suitable procurement methods. Refer to Table 7.1:

- First priority is time certainty, and the table gives four possibilities: traditional or project management competitive, design and build, or management contracting.

- There are two contenders for second priority: time economy and design quality. The first is probably best served by design and build or management contracting, the second by any form of traditional or project management or by design and manage. There is an immediate conflict and it may be necessary to decide between the two criteria, but at this point it is best to proceed matching criteria to the table, marking on the weightings as indicated in Fig. 7.4. The easiest way to do this is to cover the table with tracing paper.

- By simply adding the weightings together, the procurement methods which score highest are either traditional or project management by competitive tender.

- These two methods have only an average rating as far as the high priority time economy and low priority control – risk to the contractor is concerned. Ignore the low priority criterion and see which procurement methods are

**7.3** Worked examples

most suitable for time economy. There are just two in the table: design and build or management contracting. But design and build scores badly in terms of suitability for complex buildings and cost economy, and has only average suitability in terms of quality of design and construction. Management contracting scores badly on cost economy, cost certainty and control – risk to the contractor.

- At this stage, therefore, a priority decision must be made between quality of design or time economy. For this purpose, we will assume that quality of design is considered to be most important.

**Table 7.3** Procurement methods and forms of contract

| Forms of contract | Traditional • Competitive | Traditional • Negotiated/ two-stage | Project management • Competitive | Project management • Negotiated/ two-stage | Design and manage | Design and build | Management contracting | Construction management |
|---|---|---|---|---|---|---|---|---|
| JCT 80 With Quantities | ● | ● | ● | ● | – | – | – | – |
| JCT 80 With Approximate Quantities | ● | ● | ● | ● | – | – | – | – |
| JCT 80 Without Quantities | ● | ● | – | – | – | – | – | – |
| IFC 84 Intermediate Form | ● | ● | – | – | – | – | – | – |
| MW80 Minor Works Form | ● | – | – | – | – | – | – | – |
| JCT 81 With Contractor's Design | – | – | – | – | – | ● | – | – |
| JCT Fixed Fee Form | – | – | – | – | – | – | ● | – |
| JCT 87 Management Contract | – | – | ● | – | – | – | ● | – |
| ACA 2 | ● | ● | ● | ● | – | ● | – | – |
| ASI | ● | ● | – | – | – | – | – | – |
| ASI SW | ● | – | – | – | – | – | – | – |
| ASI MW | ● | – | – | – | – | – | – | – |

7   Choice of contract

The next stage is to make a rough choice of contract on the basis of Fig. 7.2. The choice appears to be between JCT 80 With Quantities or ACA 2 with a possibility of JCT 87 if early completion or changes during the building period are envisaged. Checking the criteria on Table 7.2, all three contracts appear suitable.

Checking procurement methods against forms of contract on Table 7.3, the choice narrows between JCT 80 With Quantities, and ACA 2.

**Fig. 7.3**

Example 7.3.1.

| Criteria | Importance | | | | | | | | | | | |
|---|---|---|---|---|---|---|---|---|---|---|---|---|
| | Very | | | | | | | | | | | Not |
| | 12 | 11 | 10 | 9 | 8 | 7 | 6 | 5 | 4 | 3 | 2 | 1 |
| • Time | | | | | | | | | | | | |
|   -Economy | | | x | | | | | | | | | |
|   -Certainty | x | | | | | | | | | | | |
| • Cost | | | | | | | | | | | | |
|   -Economy | | | | x | | | | | | | | |
|   -Certainty | | | x | | | | | | | | | |
| • Control | | | | | | | | | | | | |
|   -Risk to employer | | | | | | | | | | | | |
|   -Risk to contractor | | | | x | | | | | | | | |
| • Quality | | | | | | | | | | | | |
|   -Design | | | x | | | | | | | | | |
|   -Construction | | | x | | | | | | | | | |
| • Size/value | | | | | | | | | | | | |
|   -Medium–large | | | | | x | | | | | | | |
|   -Small–medium | | | | | | | | | | | | |
| • Complexity | | | | | | | | | | | | |
|   -Complex | | | | | x | | | | | | | |
|   -Simple | | | | | | | | | | | | |

**7.3 Worked examples**

**Fig. 7.4**

Choosing procurement methods from criteria.

| Procurement criteria | Traditional • Competitive | Traditional • Negotiated/two stage | Project management • Competitive | Project management • Negotiated/two-stage | Design and manage | Design and build | Management contracting | Construction management |
|---|---|---|---|---|---|---|---|---|
| Time • Economy | - | - | - | - | - | 11 | 11 | - |
| Time • Certainty | 12 | - | 12 | - | - | 12 | 12 | - |
| Cost • Economy | 9 | - | 9 | - | - | - | - | - |
| Cost • Certainty | 10 | 10 | 10 | 10 | - | 10 | - | - |
| Control • Risk to employer | - | - | - | - | - | - | - | - |
| Control • Risk to contractor | - | - | - | - | 9 | 9 | - | - |
| Quality • Design | 11 | 11 | 11 | 11 | 11 | - | - | - |
| Quality • Construction | - | 10 | - | 10 | - | - | 10 | 10 |
| Size/value • Medium–large | 8 | 8 | 8 | 8 | 8 | 8 | 8 | 8 |
| Size/value • Small–medium | - | - | - | - | - | - | - | - |
| Complexity • Complex | 8 | 8 | 8 | 8 | - | - | 8 | 8 |
| Complexity • Simple | - | - | - | - | - | - | - | - |
| Totals: | 58 | 47 | 58 | 47 | 28 | 50 | 49 | 26 |

Now is the time to look closely at the criteria in relation to the key provisions in Chapter 6. The tables provide useful checks. Since time certainty is the priority, ACA 2 using the first alternative of clause 11.5 would appear most suitable because it confines the grounds for extension to the essential actions and omissions and so on of the employer. This puts the risk of delay for all other reasons on the contractor. It may increase the cost somewhat, but that is relatively low priority. Both contracts make provision for sectional completion (JCT 80 by means of the supplement), so the choice falls narrowly on ACA 2 in this instance.

The next stage is to look quickly through section 5.10 dealing with ACA 2. There appear to be no problems. In this instance, therefore, ACA 2 is a suitable contract form based on the criteria and priorities noted above.

### 7.3.2 Example

A developer with little cash available to tie up for long periods wishes to refurbish some old city centre warehouses as small office units for which he perceives a demand. The key elements of the brief are:

- Completion (shells only plus services) is required as quickly as possible. The actual completion date is not significant.
- The building must be as inexpensive as possible.
- The quality of design must be as good and fashionable as can be achieved for no extra 'design costs'.
- The quality of construction must be adequate.
- The project is in the category medium to large: £1/2 to 1 million.
- The project is simple in scope with few specialists.

**Fig. 7.5**
Example 7.3.2.

| Criteria | Importance |||||||||||| |
|---|---|---|---|---|---|---|---|---|---|---|---|---|
| | Very | | | | | | | | | | | Not |
| | 12 | 11 | 10 | 9 | 8 | 7 | 6 | 5 | 4 | 3 | 2 | 1 |
| **Time** | | | | | | | | | | | | |
| -Economy | | | x | | | | | | | | | |
| -Certainty | | | | | | | | | | | | |
| **Cost** | | | | | | | | | | | | |
| -Economy | | | | x | | | | | | | | |
| -Certainty | | | | | | x | | | | | | |
| **Control** | | | | | | | | | | | | |
| -Risk to employer | | | | | | | | | | | | |
| -Risk to contractor | | | | | | | | x | | | | |
| **Quality** | | | | | | | | | | | | |
| -Design | | | | | | | x | | | | | |
| -Construction | | | | | | | x | | | | | |
| **Size/value** | | | | | | | | | | | | |
| -Medium–large | | | | | | | | | | | x | |
| -Small–medium | | | | | | | | | | | | |
| **Complexity** | | | | | | | | | | | | |
| -Complex | | | | | | | | | | | | |
| -Simple | | | | | | | | | | | x | |

**7.3** Worked examples

Following the appropriate processes may give a set of weightings similar to those indicated in Fig. 7.5. The choice is between a traditional or design and build procurement system. Working through the methodology produces a clear choice between JCT 81 and JCT 80 With Quantities. Detailed checks of Tables 7.2, 7.3 and Chapters 5 and 6 reinforce the view. Discussion with the developer will no doubt emphasise the importance of a very quick turnover and design and build using JCT 81 will produce a building very quickly, satisfying all the criteria except the ability to produce the cheapest cost. Against that must be set the certainty of cost.

**Fig. 7.6**
Example 7.3.3.

| Criteria | Importance Very | 12 | 11 | 10 | 9 | 8 | 7 | 6 | 5 | 4 | 3 | 2 | 1 Not |
|---|---|---|---|---|---|---|---|---|---|---|---|---|---|
| **• Time** | | | | | | | | | | | | | |
| -Economy | | | | x | | | | | | | | | |
| -Certainty | | | | | | | | | | | | | |
| **• Cost** | | | | | | | | | | | | | |
| -Economy | | | | | x | | | | | | | | |
| -Certainty | | | | | x | | | | | | | | |
| **• Control** | | | | | | | | | | | | | |
| -Risk to employer | | | | | | | | | | | | | |
| -Risk to contractor | | | | | | | x | | | | | | |
| **• Quality** | | | | | | | | | | | | | |
| -Design | | | | | x | | | | | | | | |
| -Construction | | | | | x | | | | | | | | |
| **• Size/value** | | | | | | | | | | | | | |
| -Medium–large | | | | | | | | | | | | x | |
| -Small–medium | | | | | | | | | | | | | |
| **• Complexity** | | | | | | | | | | | | | |
| -Complex | | | | | | | | | | | | | |
| -Simple | | | | | | | | | | x | | | |

7 Choice of contract

### 7.3.3 Example

A local authority is anxious to construct a new housing estate to relieve its housing shortage. The key elements in the brief are:

- Completion must be achieved as quickly as possible with the ability to move tenants into some houses before the whole estate is completed.
- The estate must be constructed as cheaply as possible, but the overriding principle is one of 'value for money'.
- Good design and construction standards are required to keep maintenance costs within reasonable limits.
- Few specialists will be employed as sub-contractors.
- The project is relatively large with a total contract sum of about £5 million.

Following the appropriate processes may give a set of weightings similar to those in Fig. 7.6. The procurement choice is between traditional competitive and design and build. If speed is not considered the top priority, the preferred system is traditional competitive. If the local authority wishes to use its own architects and quantity surveyors, the procurement system is confirmed. Checking Tables 7.1 and 7.3 reveals that JCT 80 With Quantities and Sectional Completion Supplement or ACA 2 are suitable forms and this is confirmed by checking Chapters 5 and 6. ACA 2 imposes a strict discipline on all parties, and unless all drawings can be programmed before the contract is executed, JCT 80 is probably most suitable.

### 7.3.4 Example

A large hotel group wishes to refurbish one of its town centre hotels in the Midlands. The key elements in its requirements are:

- Trade must be allowed to continue throughout the work, therefore, phasing and re-arrangement of work areas are necessary according to a strict programme.
- Speed is essential.
- Since the hotel must be ready in time for the tourist season, the completion date must be reasonably certain although one or two weeks overrun may not be critical.
- Price is not of prime importance and there may be a considerable quantity of work which cannot be foreseen until work commences.
- First-class quality is required.
- Services are quite complex.
- The contract sum is approximately £3–4 million.
- The project is fairly complex.

**7.3** Worked examples

The priorities might be similar to the pattern in Fig. 7.7. The clear favourite system of procurement, using the method set out in the first example, is management contracting. The only available form is JCT 87, but when Fig. 7.2 is consulted it appears that JCT 80 With Approximate Quantities is most suitable. Checking with Chapters 5 and 6 confirms that either form will be suitable if the sectional or phased completion supplement is used to deal with the strict timetable required. Most of the risk falls on the employer if management contracting is chosen, and the cost may be higher than if a traditional system is used, but the criteria suggest that the employer is willing to take the risk, and pay slightly more to obtain the benefits of early start and completion and tight controls on quality. If a great deal of additional work is revealed when work is in progress, the management contract option provides for acceleration measures.

**Fig. 7.7**
Example 7.3.4.

| Criteria | | Importance | | | | | | | | | | | |
|---|---|---|---|---|---|---|---|---|---|---|---|---|---|
| | Very | | | | | | | | | | | Not | |
| | 12 | 11 | 10 | 9 | 8 | 7 | 6 | 5 | 4 | 3 | 2 | 1 | |
| • Time | | | | | | | | | | | | | |
| -Economy | | x | | | | | | | | | | | |
| -Certainty | | | | x | | | | | | | | | |
| • Cost | | | | | | | | | | | | | |
| -Economy | | | | | | | | | | x | | | |
| -Certainty | | | | | | | | | | | | | |
| • Control | | | | | | | | | | | | | |
| -Risk to employer | | | | | x | | | | | | | | |
| -Risk to contractor | | | | | | | | | x | | | | |
| • Quality | | | | | | | | | | | | | |
| -Design | | | x | | | | | | | | | | |
| -Construction | | | x | | | | | | | | | | |
| • Size/value | | | | | | | | | | | | | |
| -Medium–large | | | | | | | | | | | x | | |
| -Small–medium | | | | | | | | | | | | | |
| • Complexity | | | | | | | | | | | | | |
| -Complex | | | | | | | | x | | | | | |
| -Simple | | | | | | | | | | | | | |

7   Choice of contract

### 7.3.5 Example

A local authority, in partnership with local business interests, is to construct a very large shopping/leisure complex. The key elements in the criteria are:

- The complex must be open in time for the city's centenary celebrations.
- High quality design and construction is required.
- Value for money rather than rock bottom cost is required.
- The contract sum will be £35–40 million.
- The employer is happy to take all the risk in return for complete control of the project.
- The project is extremely complex.

Suggested priorities are shown in Fig. 7.8. When put into Table 7.1 the suggested procurement system is management contracting. JCT 87 is indicated as the appropriate contract and cross checks to the other tables and Chapters 5 and 6 reveal nothing to change this conclusion.

**Fig. 7.8**
Example 7.3.5.

| Criteria | Importance | | | | | | | | | | | |
|---|---|---|---|---|---|---|---|---|---|---|---|---|
| | Very | | | | | | | | | | | Not |
| | 12 | 11 | 10 | 9 | 8 | 7 | 6 | 5 | 4 | 3 | 2 | 1 |
| **Time** | | | | | | | | | | | | |
| -Economy | | | | | | x | | | | | | |
| -Certainty | x | | | | | | | | | | | |
| **Cost** | | | | | | | | | | | | |
| -Economy | | | | | x | | | | | | | |
| -Certainty | | | | | | | | | | | | |
| **Control** | | | | | | | | | | | | |
| -Risk to employer | | | | x | | | | | | | | |
| -Risk to contractor | | | | | | | | | | | | |
| **Quality** | | | | | | | | | | | | |
| -Design | | | | | x | | | | | | | |
| -Construction | | | | | x | | | | | | | |
| **Size/value** | | | | | | | | | | | | |
| -Medium–large | | | | | | | x | | | | | |
| -Small–medium | | | | | | | | | | | | |
| **Complexity** | | | | | | | | | | | | |
| -Complex | | | | | | x | | | | | | |
| -Simple | | | | | | | | | | | | |

**7.3  Worked examples**

### 7.3.6 Example

A developer wishes to erect a group of six identical industrial units. The key criteria are:

- Erection must be quick.
- The cost must be cheap.
- Cost is expected to be about £3 million.
- Construction must be adequate, but design is not important.
- The buildings will be relatively simple shells.
- Phased completion will be required for leasing purposes.

**Fig. 7.9**
Example 7.3.6.

| Criteria | Importance |||||||||||||
|---|---|---|---|---|---|---|---|---|---|---|---|---|
| | Very | | | | | | | | | | | Not |
| | 12 | 11 | 10 | 9 | 8 | 7 | 6 | 5 | 4 | 3 | 2 | 1 |
| **Time** | | | | | | | | | | | | |
| -Economy | x | | | | | | | | | | | |
| -Certainty | | | | | | | | | | | | |
| **Cost** | | | | | | | | | | | | |
| -Economy | | x | | | | | | | | | | |
| -Certainty | | | | | | | | | | | | |
| **Control** | | | | | | | | | | | | |
| -Risk to employer | | | | | | | | | | | | |
| -Risk to contractor | | | | | x | | | | | | | |
| **Quality** | | | | | | | | | | | | |
| -Design | | | | | | | | | x | | | |
| -Construction | | | | | | x | | | | | | |
| **Size/value** | | | | | | | | | | | | |
| -Medium–large | | | | | x | | | | | | | |
| -Small–medium | | | | | | | | | | | | |
| **Complexity** | | | | | | | | | | | | |
| -Complex | | | | | | | | | | | | |
| -Simple | | | x | | | | | | | | | |

Fig. 7.9 shows suggested priorities. The indications are that design and build will suit the criteria better than other options because of the importance of speed and the simple content of the work. Design and build projects are not usually the cheapest option, and if cheapness is now seen to be the controlling factor, some other procurement system such as traditional or project management with competitive tendering would probably be better. Design and build can be made competitive and thus a cheaper price obtained at the expense of some time loss. This might be the best option in this case. Fig. 7.3 shows that the choice lies between JCT 81 and ACA 2. Since phasing is required, ACA 2 is the obvious choice because JCT 81 has no provision for phasing in the standard form; however, another option is to use JCT 81 with a special amendment drafted to deal with phasing.

**Fig. 7.10**
Example 7.3.7.

| Criteria | Importance<br>Very | | | | | | | | | | Not | |
|---|---|---|---|---|---|---|---|---|---|---|---|---|
| | 12 | 11 | 10 | 9 | 8 | 7 | 6 | 5 | 4 | 3 | 2 | 1 |
| • Time | | | | | | | | | | | | |
| -Economy | | | | | | | | | | | | |
| -Certainty | | | | | | | | | | | | |
| • Cost | | | | | | | | | | | | |
| -Economy | | | | x | | | | | | | | |
| -Certainty | | | x | | | | | | | | | |
| • Control | | | | | | | | | | | | |
| -Risk to employer | | | | | | | | | | | | |
| -Risk to contractor | | | | | x | | | | | | | |
| • Quality | | | | | | | | | | | | |
| -Design | | | | | | | x | | | | | |
| -Construction | | | | | | | x | | | | | |
| • Size/value | | | | | | | | | | | | |
| -Medium–large | | | | | | | | | | | | |
| -Small–medium | | | | | | x | | | | | | |
| • Complexity | | | | | | | | | | | | |
| -Complex | | | | | | | | | | | | |
| -Simple | | x | | | | | | | | | | |

**7.3  Worked examples**

### 7.3.7 Example

A middle-aged married couple require an extension to their house for a double garage with accommodation over for an elderly parent. The key criteria are:

- Cheapness is important, but more important is certainty of price.
- Design, construction and finishes must be of good quality.
- The project is simple with no complex services.
- The cost is likely to be £25,000–£35,000.
- Speed is important.

The priorities are shown in Fig. 7.10. A traditional competitive procurement system is indicated by Table 3.8. Flowchart 7.3 suggests that either MW 80 or ASI SW is suitable. Checking through Chapter 6 it is clear that both forms are defective in the extension of time provisions, ASI SW more so than MW 80. ASI SW has a bills of quantities option which is unlikely to be used in this instance. Familiarity or the fact that it is negotiated or the better arbitration provisions might favour MW 80, but it is probable that either form would suffice for this kind of work.

### 7.3.8 Conclusion

The above examples are merely by way of illustrating the methodology suggested in this book. In practice, the variety of criteria are limitless and here it must be stressed that quite different results will be obtained depending on the weightings given to the criteria. Hence the importance of carefully examining Table 7.3 and cross checking the results against the other figures. The weightings will be subjective except in very few instances.

**7.4**
**Some problems emphasised**

### 7.4.1 Weighting

Not all the factors which will influence the choice of procurement system and the choice of contract will be of equal weight. There will be priorities. Some of these priorities will be subjective, as perceived by the client; some may be said to be objective, as determined by the consultant concerned. Even an objective priority, however, will be a matter of the consultant's judgement and clearly experts can and do disagree.

In suggesting that priorities are given, therefore, it is accepted that the likelihood of attaining the optimum set of priorities is remote, but some priorities must be established, if not at the beginning of the exercise, then before it is completed. The weightings, therefore, have been simply suggested in order. No attempt has been made to introduce subtler weightings, to show, for example, that certainty as regards time is six and a half times as important to a particular client as quality. In practice, it is much more likely that the client will express his requirement for both criteria to be satisfied and it will be very difficult to get him to choose between them. In practice also, it is extremely unlikely that you would be in the position of having to recommend a contract which allowed for one, but not the other.

A further problem is that the client's priorities may change between the date you recommend a form of contract for use and the date work starts on site. Indeed, some would say that such a change of mind is inevitable. It is important, therefore, to confirm to your client in writing the basis on which you have recommended a particular form and to advise your client that any subsequent changes in priorities may not be capable of accommodation under the form chosen.

### 7.4.2 Not mechanical

Although this book is liberally sprinkled with flowcharts and tables, the process of contract choice is not entirely mechanical; judgement is also required at key points. These points have been made clear in the text. The tables and flowcharts will, like computers, give answers no better than the information put in. Since any mistakes will be made in circumstances where judgement is required, reducing the necessity for such judgement will reduce the chances of mistakes.

The system set out in this book is merely the codifying of the mental process that should be carried out even if you had a thoroughly detailed knowledge of all the main standard forms of contract. In this book, the tables and summarizing chapters take the place of such thorough knowledge. The flowcharts show the suggested procedures for arriving at the most appropriate answers.

### 7.4.3 The process

It should not be expected that running through the methodology as set in section 7.3 will unerringly result in the most appropriate form immediately. The process is designed to allow the user to fall back from time to time so that the system becomes a kind of forward selection/backwards elimination.

**7.5 Some possible amendments**

### 7.5.1 Priority of documents

There are dangers in making amendments, as explained in Chapter 1. You should only consider amendments as a last resort. Amending a standard form is a job for an expert. Most standard forms state a priority for the documents which go to make up the contract bundle. For example, JCT 80, in clause 2.2.1, states that nothing contained in the bills of quantities shall override or modify that which is contained in the printed form. The courts have recognised the effectiveness of this clause in several cases. This means that if, as is very common, you make amendments to the printed form and the amendments are solely contained in the preliminaries to the bills of quantities, they will not override the printed form.

Amendments which simply add to what is contained in the printed form may stay in the preliminaries, but amendments which truly amend must be inserted in the printed form itself. A common mistake is to put the amendment in the preliminaries prefaced by the words 'Notwithstanding clause 2.2.1, the following shall apply:'. This is an attempt to modify clause 2.2.1. As such, it is ineffective unless the modification is made in the printed form.

Some architects or quantity surveyors will strike out clause 2.2.1 in JCT 80 so that the preliminaries clauses will take precedence. It is true that, without an express clause to the contrary, 'type prevails over print'. The practical result, however, is likely to be massive disputes about the validity of conflicting provisions.

### 7.5.2 Discrepancies

Most of the standard forms contain provisions that if the contractor finds any discrepancies in or between the contract or other documents, he must notify the architect. It is now established that the contractor has no duty to find mistakes, only to report them if he finds them. In consequence, many architects and quantity surveyors are introducing an additional clause requiring the contractor to examine the drawings carefully and find errors.

Now it is a basic principle that two parties may enter into contract on virtually any terms they see fit (provided there is no illegality) and the courts will not interfere to save them from themselves. But where there is a standard form (JCT 63) whose provisions have been clearly and sensibly interpreted by the courts, it will probably require very clear and unambiguous words in any supplementary clause to supplant that interpretation. The amendment, if it is to be made, must be in the printed form and the courts will interpret any ambiguity in the result against the employer.

### 7.5.3 Instructions

The provisions relating to instructions are tempting for the amender. They vary widely from form to form. Amendments may cover oral instructions, empowering provisions, confirmation of instructions and provisions if instructions are not carried out. You should beware clauses such as 'The architect may issue instructions about any matter whatsoever'. They tend to be construed very strictly and probably mean 'The architect may issue any reasonable instructions about anything which is necessary to enable the works to proceed'.

The provisions for confirming oral instructions are very complex in JCT 80. In IFC 84, oral instructions are not recognised. It is common for the JCT 80 provisions to be omitted and the IFC 84 provisions to be extended to embrace oral instructions. The danger is that the full consequences of the amendments will not be properly considered. For example, it may seem sufficient to insert a clause in IFC 84 stating that 'oral instructions must be confirmed in writing by the architect within two days'.

Considering this clause, one might ask whether the confirmation ranks as a written instruction itself. Does the confirmation mean the instruction takes effect from the date of the original instruction or from the date of the confirmation? What is the position if no confirmation is given? What if the contractor confirms in writing to the architect? MW 80 has very similar provisions. MW 80, however, should not be used for the same kind or size of project as IFC 84. Looking at the relatively small sums involved in MW 80, there is probably little point in complex disputes. The same cannot be said of IFC 84.

### 7.5.4 Master programme
JCT 80, clause 5.3.1.2 requires the contractor to provide the architect with two copies of his master programme. The ASI form, clause 4.11, has a provision to similar effect. It is advisable to insert a clause requiring a programme if the printed form has no such term and to expand the term to require the programme so that it is shown as a network analysis or precedence diagram. The traditional Gantt or bar chart may have many virtues, but it is of little assistance to any of the parties who are attempting to arrive at the appropriate time extension or to decide upon the fact and cost of disruption.

Programmes are not made contract documents under any of the standard forms, but they have value as evidence of the way in which the contractor intended to carry out the work. The great virtue of a network is that it shows the dependencies of one activity on another. Since all professionals have a duty to keep up to date with their information and techniques, this is probably one of the more essential contract amendments which enables the professional to harness the resources of the computer to the business of extensions of time and loss and/or expense.

### 7.5.5 Clerk of works

IFC 84 has one of the most sensible and straightforward clauses dealing with the clerk of works. It is clause 3.10 which states: 'The Employer shall be entitled to appoint a clerk of works whose duty shall be to act solely as an inspector on behalf of the Employer under the directions of the Architect/the Contract Administrator'. There is no nonsense about directions which are to have no effect unless confirmed within two days and then to have effect only from the date of confirmation. That provision is to be found in the clerk of works clause (12) in JCT 80.

There is no reason why a clause providing for a clerk of works should not be inserted as an amendment to any form where the provision is missing and a clerk of works is required. The golden rule must be to keep it simple. Terms which allow the clerk of works to give instructions under the contract are a recipe for trouble. The contract can only work if all instructions come from one source.

### 7.5.6 Assignment and sub-letting

Under the general law, parties to a contract may assign rights but not duties. Most forms of contract forbid assignment of the contract without consent. Very often a contractor may wish to assign his right to payment to a third party in return for money 'up front' to enable him to carry out the contract. An employer may also wish to assign his right to the completed building to another in return for payment. Indeed, if the employer is a developer, selling or leasing the building is the sole purpose of the exercise. An amendment of the contract to cater for these possibilities is sensible, depending on the circumstances.

The difference between assignment and sub-letting must be clearly understood. They are quite different concepts. Assignment is the legal transference of a right or duty from one party to another. To do this properly, a series of further contracts must be set up between the interested parties. When a party's rights and duties are transferred to another, it is termed novation. After the transfer, the original party retains no interest. For example, if there is a contract between A and B, B's rights and duties can be transferred to C. Then if C fails, C is accountable directly to A. If A fails, he is accountable directly to C. Sub-letting is delegation. A duty can be sub-let with consent to a third party and the original party remains responsible for the correct performance of that duty. For example, if there is a contract between A and B, B may sub-let his duties to C. But if C fails, he is accountable to B who always remains accountable to A. If A fails, it only affects B. B remains accountable to C.

Although most standard forms state that sub-letting is possible with consent which must not be unreasonably delayed or withheld, the reality of building today is that most projects are carried out with a high proportion of sub-contractors. The favourite type of amendment is to JCT 80 clause 19.3, the 'listing' provisions. It seems to be the misapprehension that if the clause is altered so that a list of one firm is included, this will overcome the problems of nomination. In such cases the amender fails to realise that to name only one person in the bills of quantities amounts to nomination under the terms of clause 35.1. This is a clause which should not be amended.

### 7.5.7 Possession, deferment and completion

Failure on the part of the employer to give possession is a serious breach of contract unless deferment provisions apply. It is important, therefore, to ensure that if deferment provisions are included in the contract, they do apply and if such provisions are not included, some deferment provisions are inserted. Few contracts include for deferment lasting longer than six weeks, but there is no reason, other than a higher tender figure, why you should not arrange to have the length of deferment period extended to whatever you consider may be necessary. Alternatively, if you are aware that possession may be delayed, it is wise to put a realistic date in the contract.

Problems can be caused for the employer if the contractor finishes earlier than the contract completion date. Most standard forms specifically allow early completion, for example clause 2.1 of IFC 84 states that the contractor must 'regularly and diligently proceed with the Works and shall complete the same on or before the Date for Completion stated in the Appendix'.

Of course it is a comparatively easy matter to amend the clause to state 'on *but not before* the Date for Completion'. That will probably prevent the contractor completing before completion date and necessitate the architect issuing a certificate of practical completion with all that it involves. Unfortunately, even if the amendment is in place it does not solve the problem of cash flow. If a contract is to be complete in a fifteen month period and the contractor finishes in ten months except for a few trifling items which the contractor can play

**7.5**   Some possible amendments

with until he is expected to complete, the employer may be severely embarrassed by having to find money much earlier than he anticipated. Any amendment to deal with this problem is likely to be very complex.

### 7.5.8 Extension of time

On no account must any amendment be made to JCT 80 clause 25 unless amendments are also made to the fluctuations clause. Otherwise, fluctuations would not be frozen if the contractor is in default. It is also important that no amendments are made to any extension of time clause which have the effect of removing the architect's power to give an extension for an act of omission or default of the employer or the architect.

The general law is clear that the contractor's obligation to complete the works by the contract completion date is removed if the employer or his agent prevent such completion by interference or hindrance. Liquidated damages could not then be applied because there would be no date from which they could run. Therefore, although you may consider omitting some of the grounds for extension, it is essential that the grounds cover any acts which could be said to be the fault of the employer. In this respect, you might consider increasing the grounds if any occur to you which are not covered in the contract.

### 7.5.9 Loss and/or expense

Some professionals have been known to advise deleting the whole of the loss and/or expense provisions in a standard form. The basis seems to be that the contractor will just have to take the risk and price for it. Nothing could be further from the truth. To have a loss and/or expense clause means that the contractor can recover his additional costs and loss directly caused by certain specified matters listed in the contract. If there is no machinery available in the contract, the contractor is simply thrown onto his common law remedies, i.e. mainly damages for breach of contract, in respect of his direct loss and/or expense.

It is obviously better to have the means for settling such matters without resorting to legal proceedings. Clauses can be inserted which impose time limits on the parties, but even where there is a loss and/or expense clause in the contract, there is nothing to prevent the contractor seeking his common law remedies instead of, or as well as, taking the contractual route, therefore, any attempt to make life more difficult for a contractor who has a valid claim for loss and/or expense is probably self-defeating.

### 7.5.10 Nomination

The complexity of the nomination clause in JCT 80 has led many professionals to delete it altogether. If this meant that all work would be specified or measured in detail, there would be few complaints. Usually, however, the deletion of the nomination clause is accompanied by wholesale amendment of the sub-letting clause in an attempt to create a nomination clause which is not a nomination clause. It must be said that this kind of exercise is fraught with problems and invariably leads to trouble. A variant is where bits from other standard forms are lifted out of context and inserted into the standard form under consideration.

It is tempting to say that if the employer does not want nominated sub-contractors, he should use another standard form. However, he probably does want nominated sub-contractors, but without the consequences. Once a sub-contractor is nominated, there is no escaping the consequences.

### 7.5.11 Time periods

Time periods are a favourite subject of amendments. Most common is to extend the period for honouring certificates. This is a grave disadvantage to the contractor and it should only be done if it is really necessary. If it is done simply so that the employer can have the use of the money longer, the contractor should insert an interest charge in his tender.

ACA 2 standard form has provision for all the time periods to be altered. It is particularly useful with this form because the periods already in the form tend to be rather short. It is of course essential that wherever a time period is amended, all similar or relevant time periods are also amended.

# Bibliography

Ashworth, A. (1987) *Contractual Procedures in the Construction Industry*, Longman.

Bennett, J. (1985) *Construction Project Management*, Architectural Press.

Bowyer, J. (1986) *Small Works Contract Documentation*, Architectural Press.

Chappell, D. (1989) ASI Forms of Contract, *Architects' Journal*, 22 March to 12 April.

Chappell, D. (1990) *Contractual Correspondence for Architects*, 2nd edn, Legal Studies and Services.

Chappell, D. (1991) *Understanding JCT Contracts*, International Thomson Publishing.

Chappell, D. and Powell-Smith, V. (1990) *JCT Intermediate Form of Contract – A Practical Guide*, 2nd edn, Legal Studies and Services.

Chappell, D. and Powell-Smith, V. (1990) *JCT Minor Works Form of Contract – A Practical Guide*, 2nd edn, Legal Studies and Services.

Clamp, H. and Cox, S. (1989) *Which Contract?* RIBA Publications.

Cox, S. (1989) *The Architect's Guide to the JCT Intermediate Form of Building Contract*, 2nd edn, RIBA Publications.

Dearle and Henderson (1988) *Management Contracting – A Practice Manual.*

Franks, J. and Harlow, P. (1984) *Building Procurement Systems – A Guide to Building Project Management*, CIOB.

Green, R. (1986) *The Architect's Guide to Running a Job*, 4th edn, Architectural Press.

Keating, D. (1978) *Building Contracts*, with suppl., Sweet and Maxwell.

Marsh, P. D. V. (1984) *Contract Negotiation Handbook*, Gower Press.

Parris, J. (1988) *Making Commercial Contracts*, Blackwell.

Powell-Smith, V. and Chappell, D. (1990) *Building Contracts Compared and Tabulated*, 2nd edn, Legal Studies and Services.

Powell-Smith, V. and Chappell, D. (1990) *Building Contract Dictionary*, 2nd edn, Legal Studies and Services.

Powell-Smith, V. and Furmston, M. P. (1989) *Building Contract Casebook*, 2nd edn, Blackwell.

Powell-Smith, V. and Sims, J. (1989) *JCT Management Contract – A Practical Guide*, Kluwer.

Speight, A. and Stone, G. (1985) *AJ Legal Handbook*, 5th edn, Architectural Press.

Turner, D. F. (1986) *Design and Build Contract Practice*, Longman.

Wallace, I. N. D. (1970) *Hudson's Building and Civil Engineering Contracts*, 10th edn (with suppl. 1979), Sweet and Maxwell.

Willis, C. J. and Ashworth, A. (1987) *Practice and Procedure for the Quantity Surveyor*, Blackwell.

Yates, A. (1982) *Exclusion Clauses in Contracts*, Sweet and Maxwell.